Kit's Kingdom:
The Journalism of
Kathleen Blake Coleman

KIT'S KINGDOM

The Journalism of
Kathleen Blake Coleman

by

Barbara M. Freeman

CARLETON UNIVERSITY PRESS
OTTAWA, CANADA
1989

©Carleton University Press Inc. 1989

ISBN   0-88629-105-4   (paperback)
        0-88629-114-3   (casebound)

Printed and bound in Canada

Carleton Women's Experience Series #1

Canadian Cataloguing in Publication Data

Freeman, Barbara M., 1947-
    Kit's Kingdom: the journalism of Kathleen Blake Coleman

ISBN 0-88629-105-4

    1. Coleman, Kit, 1864-1915. 2. Journalists—Canada—
Biography. I. Title.

PN4913.C6F73 1989   070'.92'4   C89-090354-9

Distributed by: Oxford University Press Canada
                    70 Wynford Drive,
                    Don Mills, Ontario.
                    Canada. M3C 1J9
                    (416) 441-2941

Cover Design: Robert Chitty

Acknowledgement

Carleton University Press gratefully acknowledges the support
extended to its publishing programme by the Canada Council and
the Ontario Arts Council.
This book has been published with the help of a grant from the
Canadian Federation for the Humanities, using funds provided
by the Social Sciences and Humanities Research Council of
Canada.

This book is dedicated with thanks to my mother, Marie, and to the memory of my late father, Tom (1912-1987).

Kathleen Blake Coleman, 1894 (National Archives of Canada/PA164721)

TABLE OF CONTENTS

GENERAL INTRODUCTION

One of the most interesting ongoing debates within the university world is the one which accompanies the emergence of a new discipline. It makes no difference whether the debate took place yesterday, a century ago or even further in the past, the arguments which surround the arrival of a newcomer to the academy are intricate and bitter. That upstart "History" was frowned upon in the nineteenth century as much as "Sociology" was condemned by university establishments in the early twentieth century. "Computer Science" and "Bio-chemistry" fight for attention now against as many adversaries as "Psychology" had in 1900.

The foundation of opposition to new disciplines comes from two sources: the philosophy which leads to discipline identification in the first place and the beliefs of all academics in the particular importance of the skills of their fields. A discipline, in whatever larger grouping of academic categories it be housed, is fundamentally a way of looking at the human experience. People become historians or physicists, engineers or scholars of music because the particular field chosen seems a marvellous and exciting way of learning about what is important in life. A discipline is a statement that this particular perception, whether it be the examination of the planet, as in earth sciences or the examination of the past, as in history, is a most useful, intelligent, intelligible, way of understanding that which is. For many people in many disciplines their subject is the only fully reasonable, intelligent and rational way of looking at the universe. Any proposal to suggest a new basic ground of investigation is subject to intense questioning.

At the same time, each discipline has evolved methods of investigation and a rationale of theory which defines its own particular standards of academic excellence. Each discipline not only considers the world from a particular angle – it also considers some particular methods of thinking and communication as better than others. As well as a philosophy of knowledge, each discipline also has its own craft. New disciplines must prove not only that the angle of perception advanced is a coherent and intelligible approach to the study of worthwhile matters, but that the methods it wants to use are the proper tools for the task.

It is not, therefore, surprising that the field of women's studies in general and feminist theory in particular has had a battle for acceptance. It is yet one more attempt to expand the number of ways in which research and teaching shall be organised within the academy. And it is also a challenge to many of the practices of nature of the established disciplines themselves. On a very basic level there is the challenge to the competence of existing scholarship: women's studies implies that to write without due recognition of the existence and importance of women is to be incompetent. Then there is a challenge to the objectivity of research: to take for granted, without examination, that the experience of the male is the norm and that of the female the variant, not only suggests bias but can be shown to vitiate the results of the work. Margrit Eichler's outstanding examination of sexism as a component in academic judgement has made uncomfortable reading for people whose professional code is based upon a desire for impartial judgement, dispassionate and unprejudiced examination of evidence.[1]

In sum, the emergence of women's studies has meant that the academy is asked to consider the possibility not only of one more place of perception for an intelligible view of life, but also the fact that this new discipline's very existence will mean a continuous critical light upon the work of those already established. It is the overwhelming importance of this challenge which has led Carleton University Press to establish the series in *Women's Experience.*

It is hoped that the works which will form the series will help to clarify many of the questions which women's studies advocates must answer. The editor of the series will be looking for books which illustrate the dual nature of women's studies and feminist theory. Works rooted in the examination of the ways in which particular women have experienced the impact of gender definition are needed as much as those which analyse the links between feminist theory and general patterns of analysis proposed by the established university disciplines. The reality of women's lives has to be made explicit and, at the same time, the assumptions about the proper relationships of men and women must be examined. It is expected that the volumes published in the series will address such issues as the following: when is gender a useful tool of analysis? When does it matter that a human is female rather than male? Why, by whom and in what circumstances is the decision made that this distinction is important? What issues are involved in the translation of a human's sexual character into particular modes of social expectation?

It is perhaps necessary, at this stage in the evolution of women's studies to state explicitly that not all books by women are works that should be considered part of such a series. Those works which turn upon particular experiences of women need to have the context of gender analysis as part of the intellectual structure of the work.

It is a particular pleasure to see that the opening volume is a work which makes clear this distinction. Barbara Freeman's life of Kit Coleman presents the problems of women's studies and feminist theory in all their complexity by concentrating on what is apparently a very simple issue: what did it mean to her subject that she was a woman and not a man? Carleton University Press is delighted to open this new venture with such a fine study.

N.E.S. Griffiths

Department of History
Carleton University
November 1989

Notes

1. The text of this work has been published in a number of places but the reference for the most readily available form can be had from Canadian research Institute for the Advancement of Women.

PREFACE

Kathleen Blake Coleman a.k.a Catherine Ferguson Willis (1856-1915) arrived in Canada a well-educated but destitute Irish immigrant in 1884. To earn her living and support her two Canadian-born children, she juggled the androgynous and womanly aspects of her character to invent an intriguing public persona designed to draw readers of both sexes: "Kit" of the Toronto Daily *Mail/Mail and Empire*.

Although she was initially hired to lure female readers with timely and entertaining articles on household matters and fashion, she escaped the confines of her "Woman's Kingdom" page whenever she could and eventually became internationally famous as an adventurous travel writer and war correspondent (Spanish-American War of 1898). She was never an advocate of armed conflict, however, and devoted many angry, sad and blunt words to its evils.

In private life, she was a mother-journalist painfully trying to balance her domestic duties and her own literary ambition. Her experiences of life made her quick to sympathize with others, especially working women of all kinds, but her liberalism had its limits. She believed in the intellectual and economic equality of the sexes and helped other women succeed in journalism. But for professional and personal reasons, she remained aloof from the women's movement itself and did not openly advocate suffrage until it became a respectable cause.

ACKNOWLEDGEMENTS

This book has been a rite of passage from the daily news broadcaster I was ten years ago to the academic journalist I have become. It has been an exciting journey, one that is not nearly finished. While I take responsibility for the contents of this book, I would like to thank the colleagues and friends who have directly contributed to it, most of them at Carleton University.

In the Department of History: Professor Deborah Gorham, my academic advisor and good friend, whose women's history courses first inspired me and whose unfailing encouragement and guidance kept me going; Carleton's former Dean of Arts, Naomi Griffiths, who has also warmly supported me in my efforts and, as interim editor of Carleton University Press, helped shape the final manuscript of this book; Professor Marilyn Barber for her valuable suggestions and Professors J.K. Johnson and Del Muise for their comments on earlier papers.

In the Institute of Canadian Studies: Professor Patricia Smart for her insightful comments and Professor Jill Vickers for her wise guidance in feminist theory (and practice.)

In the School of Journalism: I especially want to thank Professor Carman Cumming for his careful reading of an earlier version of the manuscript and a later chapter and his warm generosity in sharing his expertise on Kit's first editor at the *Daily Mail*, Edward Farrer. Several other colleagues have also helped and encouraged me in this venture, including Professors Catherine McKercher, Eileen Saunders, Ross Eaman and Professor Emeritus Wilfrid Kesterton.

At Carleton University Press: I would like to thank general editors Michael Gnarowski and David Knight, copy editor Gordon McMillan, Pauline Adams and the Press staff for their assistance along the way.

There are several people outside Carleton to whom I owe thanks, as well: Marjory Lang, PhD. and Linda Hale of Vancouver for generously sharing with me some of their own findings on the early Canadian women journalists; Professor Misao Dean of the Department of English at the University of Victoria for her thoughtful comments and interest in my work; Professor Susan Henry of the Department of Journalism at the University of California (Northridge), editor of *Journalism History*, whose constructive criticisms of an earlier version of Kit's adventures in Cuba contributed substantially to that chapter; Mike Musick of the National Archives of the United States in Washington, D.C. and David Fraser and Joan Schwartz of the National Archives of Canada in Ottawa for their help with the research the book entailed; and my good friends (and cheering section) Diane Kilby, Anne Whitehurst, Sally Swenson and Andrea Nugent, who helped check the proofs.

I would also like to thank Kathleen Blake Coleman's descendants, Kit Waterous of Brantford, Ont. and J.B. Gartshore of Ancaster, Ont., for their kindness in providing vital information and material on the Coleman family.

My thanks also to my family for their love, encouragement and pride in my accomplishments. I am especially grateful to Gabriella Goliger, my dearest and best companion, who has lived with me—and "Kit"—for several years and has endured us both with patience, humour and appropriate editorial comment.

B.M.F.

INTRODUCTION

On June 26, 1884, an Allan Lines steamship, the S.S. "Circassian," left Liverpool bound for Quebec, carrying about 500 passengers. Among them was a young Irish widow, Mrs. Willis, described on the passenger list as a "lady."[1] At the time, she was destitute, but she was destined to become one of Canada's most popular, colourful— and elusive—journalists.

At age twenty-eight, Mrs. Willis was a tall, slim woman with the auburn hair and brown eyes common to the Spanish-Irish people of Galway. She would not have called herself a conventional beauty,[2] having a gamine face and a rather determined chin, but she had a stately air about her and acquaintances were often struck by her intelligence, her warmth, and the musical quality of her accent. They also noticed a quiet melancholia which never seemed to leave her.[3]

Mrs. Willis had already suffered considerable hardship. Her one child, two-year-old Mary Margaret, had died and her rich husband had left her without a penny.[4] Like many Irishwomen in poor financial straits, she had left her economically depressed native land in search of a better life.[5] Since she was well educated in the classics, and knew music and several languages, she went to London where she struggled to eke out a living as a governess.[6] But the meager earnings and dull respectability were not enough for a woman who not only liked her creature comforts but was blessed with a spirit of adventure.

The night before she left London to take the boat at Liverpool, she was feted by a comically odd mix of "Bohemian" friends at her lodgings, the "French Pension for Governesses," in the Bayswater district. Or so she would write the story, in her vivid style, several years later. It was a hilarious farewell party, followed by tearful farewells on the railway station platform the following day. After the unhappy start to her adult life, she was going to Canada to begin again.[7]

For Mrs. Willis, a new life meant a new identity. She had been born Catherine Ferguson in 1856, but, for an unknown reason, had changed her name to Kathleen before her marriage.[8] By the time she had sailed the ocean to Canada, she had subtracted eight years and three months from her actual age. According to a note in her private papers, written in her hand, she was: "Little Kathleen Willis 19 years old—and feeling very, very old indeed and—lonely. Dated this day of our Lord the 14th of July 1884."[9]

In Canada, she married again—twice. Her second husband was an English ne'er do well named Edward J. Watkins, with whom she had a son and a daughter. Around the time their marriage broke up, she adopted a prestigious middle name, that of the Galway Blakes,[10] and went to work as a journalist to support herself and her children. The third husband, whom she married several years later, was a kind-hearted Canadian doctor, Theobald Coleman. Today, she is remembered as Kathleen Blake Coleman, or "Kit," an internationally known women's page writer, travel journalist and war correspondent. Her career spanned the years 1889, when she began as a freelance writer, to 1915, the year she died. For most of that time she was in charge of the "Woman's Kingdom" page in the Saturday edition of one of the major Toronto newspapers, the *Daily Mail*, which later became the *Mail and Empire*.

Kathleen Blake Coleman has several layers of identity and unravelling them has been an engaging task. My first introduction to her occurred over a decade ago, when I picked up Ted Ferguson's compilation of excerpts from her columns, *Kit Coleman: Queen of Hearts,*[11] and was immediately struck by her colourful and imaginative prose. I knew then that I wanted to explore her writing further in some way, but at the time, I was busy working as a radio journalist and had no time even to consider writing a book.

The fact that she had been one of the first women to work in the world of newspapers also intrigued me. I could relate to her experiences as I had been among the first female news reporters in Canadian broadcasting and was still greatly outnumbered by male colleagues. Role models were, and still are, important to me, and I accepted Kit as one of the earliest. My idea of her was quite romantic at the time. Not only did I view her as larger than life, I naturally—and naively—assumed that, given her experiences, she must have been a feminist like myself.

In 1980, I accepted a job teaching radio journalism at Carleton University. One of the first things that struck me was that the ratio of my female to male students—two to one—was almost directly the reverse of the status quo in most of today's newsrooms. Yet there was little in the way of journalism history, or any other aspect of their education, that directly addressed their needs as women who would be working in the field. I and several other colleagues who share the same concerns set about to change that. My chance to involve Kit in my plans occurred when I decided to take a Master's degree in Canadian Studies, using her experiences as my thesis. That's how this book began.

Although the romantic gloss has long worn off my earlier vision of her, I have learned to appreciate Coleman's skill as a writer. I have read just about everything she ever wrote during her twenty-five years as a journalist and, despite the recurring themes in much of her work and her sometimes rushed and sloppy punctuation and phrasing, I can honestly say that she has never bored me. I can't think of a greater tribute. I have laughed out loud at her jokes—to the reproving looks of other scholars in the Archives—and

3

have stealthily wiped away a tear or two at her sadder stories. I have also been angered by her dismissal of some of the feminist concerns of her day, have become elated when she championed the cause and have been puzzled and frustrated by her inconsistencies. Several women biographers have written about the intimate experience of documenting the lives and work of other women, and I became as involved with Kit as any of them did with their subjects.[12] Through it all I have learned that Kathleen Blake Coleman was a much more complex person than I had imagined when I was first introduced to her over ten years ago.

Her main claim to fame has been her adventures in Cuba during the Spanish-American conflict of 1898, where she was apparently the first woman in the world to actually be accredited as a war correspondent.[13] But that was only one of many significant episodes in her career. It has been played up over all the others not just because of what it purportedly symbolized, a giant step for women in journalism, but because war is, in newspaper parlance, "hard copy," and, as such, a male prerogative. In fact, a re-reading of her activities in Cuba shows that she played a secondary role to that of her male colleagues, consistent with women's lack of status in the profession in general.[14]

Most journalism history has a male bias; that is, it focuses mainly on the experiences of successful, white males or reflects women's experiences in the profession from a male-centered point of view,[15] emphasizing the ones who succeeded in newspaper jobs that men would normally do, while ignoring the significance of the women journalists' more routine work. Feminist journalism historians are looking at new approaches to solve this problem[16] and I wanted to make my own contribution by re-examining a prominent journalist, taking care to re-interpet her life and work in the context of the professional and social positions of the women of her day.

For some scholars it may be tempting to dismiss the more prominent women journalists as atypical, or alternately, assume that the women working in the field were all essentially the same in their attitudes and approaches to their jobs. I believe that each journalist had her individual perspective[17] and the "exceptional" ones, like Kathleen Blake Coleman, can provide many insights, especially when their work is re-examined to see what their successes in a "man's world" really entailed.

With the outstanding exception of the work of journalist Robin Rowland, who first uncovered her real identity,[18] little real research has been done on Coleman. Most existing articles include questionable biographical detail and much praise but little analysis of her writing.[19] Ferguson's book succeeded in being entertaining, and he did try to relate Coleman's work to the position of the women of her day, but his background commentary was limited and his biographical information is, because of Rowland's sleuthing, outdated.[20] The real story of her life, and her journalism as a woman writing primarily for women, have not been examined.

A complete biography is not possible because Coleman was an intensely private person and probably destroyed any diary she kept and most of her personal papers. More than once, writing as Kit, she exhorted her readers to "Burn your letters!," diaries and other private documents to avoid being exposed to scrutiny and ridicule after death.[21] She did leave some papers and photographs, but little that is revealing. The exceptions are a loving letter from her young son,[22] her correspondence with Prime Minister Wilfrid Laurier[23] and her quasi-autobiographical stories about her childhood in Ireland, including a novel which was never published.[24] A few of her private letters in other collections,[25] a biography of a famous uncle-priest[26] and an interview with her grandchildren,[27] have been helpful, but the real Kathleen remains elusive.

Given the limitations of the biographical material on her, this is not the story of Kathleen Blake Coleman, but an account of her public persona, Kit, and how she sometimes defied, but often fulfilled, the expectations of editors and the public in what she wrote for women. Much of the material is taken from "Woman's Kingdom" in the *Daily Mail/Mail and Empire* from 1889 to 1911, her syndicated "Kit's Column," which ran in several newspapers from 1911 to 1914 and "The Pedlar's Pack," which she wrote for *Canada Monthly* magazine from 1911 to 1915. For the purposes of this study, I will call the private woman Kathleen and the persona Kit, although the more well-known and established Kit became, the closer she resembled what we know of her creator.

The multi-faceted Kit was an attractive and fascinating persona for a nineteenth century audience, one who embraced several contradictory elements. She was a feisty, adventurous Irishwoman, a small-l liberal intellectual and social critic, a Conservative apologist and a warm, motherly advice-giver to what she called her "paper-children" or "shadow-children"[28] readers. In fact, in creating Kit, Kathleen walked a creative tightrope between what was acceptable for a nineteenth century woman to write and what was too daring.

Scholars who have examined women's history and women's writing in the nineteenth century agree that female writers were subject to constraints related to their roles in society, which male writers did not have to endure. In order to understand Kit, we can adopt Elaine Showalter's view that interpretations of writing by women, based on biological, linguistic or psychological factors, do not go far enough in explaining their authors' creative conflicts. Showalter advocates the cultural approach, which takes all these factors into account but includes the economic and political pressures on the woman writer as well.[29]

One hundred years ago, women's rights were severely limited in education, economics, law and social life. In order to write about these and other problems and be taken seriously, female writers have used various devices accepted by the literary establishment. Tillie Olsen describes many of these strategies, including male (or androgynous) pen-names, male heroes, writing with "objectivity" or "detach-

ment," or alternately, writing "like a woman" in order not
to threaten men:

> Being charming, entertaining, 'small', feminine when full
> development of material would require a serious or larger
> tone and treatment. Pulling away from depths and complex-
> ity. Irony, wit, the arch, instead of directness; diffuse emotion
> or detachment instead of tragedy. Avoiding seriousness alto-
> gether. Concealing intellect, analytical ability, objectivity; or
> refusing to credit that one is capable of them. Abdicating
> "male" realms, "the large," the social, the political.[30]

The description partly fits the complex Kit, who, although
certainly outspoken at times, advocated that the female journalist should "try to infuse a little of her charming femininity
into her writings..."[31] But there were other sides to her as
well. The nineteenth century journalist's job was to entertain as well as educate, and a certain amount of literary
licence and invention was acceptable, as long as it was based
on truth.[32] Kathleen presented Kit as a heroine who broke
away from gender restrictions, and here, Ellen Moers' concept of "heroism" or "literary feminism...a heroic structure for the female voice in literature" is helpful. Moers discusses acceptable female heroines in fiction including the
traveller "...who moves, who acts, who copes with vicissi-
tude and adventure" and the most "powerful" one of all,
the educator/mother.[33] They are models which fit Kit very
well, both in relation to her efforts to escape from women's
sphere in journalism through travel writing and her com-
pliance to the expectation that she would focus on "domestic" work and mothering in "Woman's Kingdom."

She was a transitional figure in Canadian journalism.
Before the 1880s, when middle-class girls were generally not
schooled as well or as long as boys, the few published
women writers in Canada were unusually well-educated
and gifted. They included the pioneer chroniclers Catherine
Parr Traill and her sister, Susanna Moodie, who were the
products of "an articulate, literary, scribbling family,
encouraged by their parents and by the resources of a siz-
able library..."[34] Later, there was Agnes Maule Machar of

Kingston, Ontario, whose clergyman father saw to her education. Under the pen-name "Fidelis," she applied her strong Christian social gospel sentiments to many economic and social problems in a number of periodicals, such as *Rose Belford's National Annual Review* and *The Week*, and in her poetry and novels.[35]

By 1891, literacy standards in Canada had risen considerably with women becoming, on average, able to read and write as well as men, particularly in urban areas.[36] At the same time, new technologies and stiff competition among North American newspapers resulted in new editorial features, including women's pages. They were not invented to improve the status of women, but to draw advertisers and readers.[37] Despite the advances of the time, women were still seen as being primarily concerned with hearth and home and newspaper editors hired female journalists, who were a decided minority in their field,[38] to write "light" articles on domestic issues, fashion notes and household hints.

The historian Paul Rutherford believes that nineteenth century editors promoted and upheld various ideologies, including the view that women's most crucial role was mothering the nation.[39] Many editors refused to believe that their female audiences were interested in weightier matters and discouraged coverage of political and social issues, unless they had a bearing on women's domestic roles. The editorial restrictions frustrated many of the educated women journalists,[40] who struggled, with varying degrees of success, to break away from the women's pages. Kit was one of them.[41]

Although she acquiesced to many of her editor's demands, she waged several battles over her preference for intellectual fare, such as politics, religion and science, over domestic content such as household hints, recipes and the latest style in hats. She once declared: "I simply detest fashions and I think it is paying us women a poor compliment to imagine we cannot take an interest in the highest and very deepest questions of the day."[42] She had some success in expanding "Woman's Kingdom" to fit this larger vision of women's concerns.

Both W.H. Kesterton and Rutherford have mistakenly stated that women's columns and pages have historically dealt with the light and trite, or as Rutherford puts it, they served "...to satisfy curiosity, to serve and entertain but little more."[43] But intelligent, educated women journalists discussed many political and social issues, including female suffrage, in their pages. To say that Kit "...furnished a great deal more gossip than argument about women's affairs— and fashions"[44] is neither correct nor fair, and the contention that she was a "lifelong opponent of suffrage"[45] is a myth.

In fact, she could be startlingly outspoken about women's rights, but she was often inconsistent in her support. Generally, she agreed with the principles behind demands for equality but often lost sight of them when criticizing the tactics activists sometimes employed. From her earliest days on the *Daily Mail*, she was an advocate of equal pay for equal work, but she scorned "masculine platform women" for years and, unlike many of her female journalist colleagues, refused to become involved in the women's movement..[46]

There were political reasons, as well as personal ones, for her stance. Most of Canada's newspapers were allied with one political party or another.[47] When the maverick *Daily Mail* merged with the Conservative organ, the *Empire*, in 1895, Kathleen, who privately preferred editorial independence,[48] tended to toe the party line as the Kit persona, despite her belief in the freedom of the press.[49] Although newspaper columnists were encouraged to advocate various causes,[50] the *Daily Mail/Mail and Empire*, did not support women's rights. Kit was affected by this policy and also upheld the essentially masculine ideal of journalistic "objectivity" as a reason why feminist journalists should not become activists.

Eventually, she openly supported female suffrage, but not before it became a respected cause célèbre. That was rather late in the day for some of her contemporaries—and for modern scholars, who have found her lack of commitment to the women's movement hard to forgive.[51]

Her attitude is easier to understand when one examines her personal circumstances, particularly her experience as an impoverished emigrant, which haunted her for most of her life, and her struggles to survive as a journalist after she arrived in Canada. She never felt safe financially, even after she married for the third time. There was no unemployment insurance to cushion an ex-journalist or her children in her day, and, in order to earn her living, she had to work hard to maintain an image that was acceptable to her primarily conservative audience. Her sense of economic insecurity affected what she wrote about politics, religion and other contentious subjects, as well as women's rights. Despite her professional success, she was self-deprecating about her talent and was afraid to risk being unemployed by being too outspoken. In fact, it is surprising that she wrote as frankly as she sometimes did. Her timidity vanished only near the end of her life, when she became daringly blunt about the jingoism gripping Canadian society after the outbreak of the First World War.

Life as a journalist was difficult and, although she would not reveal her salary, she often complained of poor pay,[52] long hours and few holidays, once equating the job of a newspaperwoman with that of a sweatshop worker.[53] The average journalist in Toronto made thirty-five to fifty dollars a week, according to Kit,[54] but it appears the real Kathleen made even less. Estimates range from a starting rate of twenty dollars a month—which forced her to do light housekeeping overtime to make ends meet[55]—to maximums of twenty-five[56] and thirty-five dollars a week.[57] To augment her income, she took on extra assignments for her newspaper[58] and wrote short stories and freelance articles for other publications.[59] She did much of her writing and extensive reading at home, often working far into the night.[60]

Kit claimed she had a retentive memory, like "a little kodak in my brain," that helped her in her work.[61] But she was often dogged by poor health, particularly bronchial ailments and eye-trouble, and depressions that lasted for weeks or months at a time.[62] Several historians have suggested that behaviour labelled mental illness, including what we now know as depression, was a symptom of gender-role conflict in the nineteenth century woman.[63] She indicated more than once that her unhappiness was the result of her inability to pursue her highest literary goal—a novel.[64] Most of her energy was devoted to keeping her job so that she could support herself and her two children.

It is difficult to know how much of Kathleen Blake Coleman's own attitudes were embodied in Kit, but it is clear that it was a struggle for her to create a "Kingdom" that was both challenging and safe for her readers and herself. The historian Carroll Smith-Rosenberg points out that the conflict between a woman's real identity and her need to fit into a male milieu— journalism in Kit's case—often results in a literary split personality:

> To speak the language of a group not one's own—for the marginal to assume the language of the politically and economically powerful, for women to adopt a male discourse.... — may entail the denial of an essential aspect of the speaker's own identity or require the careful maintenance of a dual identity.[65]

Kathleen Blake Coleman had a long and successful career in the newspaper business because she managed to create a Kit who combined intelligence, assertiveness and ambition with romantic flair, femininity and maternalism. Despite the resulting contradictions, or perhaps because of them, she became the most popular women's page writer of her generation.

Notes

1. Public Archives of Canada, Microfilm C-4533, item 48, S.S. "Circassian" passenger list, June 26, 1884.
2. She was self-deprecating about her looks. See "Woman's Kingdom," Toronto *Daily Mail*, 3 May 1890, 5.
3. See for example, J.V. MacAree, *The Fourth Column* (Toronto: Macmillan of Canada 1934), pp. 295-296.
4. The reason for the child's death is not clear. Interview with Kathleen Blake Coleman's grandchildren, J.B. Gartshore and Kit Waterous, conducted by Barbara M. Freeman at Ancaster, Ontario 7 Dec. 1987. She may have had several children by her first marriage but none survived infancy and only Mary Margaret's birth was registered. Public Archives of Canada, Kathleen Blake Coleman Papers (hereafter PAC K.B.C. Papers) MG 29, D 112, Vol. 2, File 40, genealogy.
5. Between 1850 and 1950, fifty per cent of Irish emigrants were women, forced to leave Ireland because of lack of jobs and poor marriage prospects—legacies of the Irish famine. Joseph J. Lee, "Women and the Church Since the Famine," in Margaret MacCurtain and Donncha O Corrain (eds.), *Women in Irish History* (Dublin: Arlen House, The Women's Press, 1978), 38.
6. Mary H. Krout, "A Canadian Journalist" in *The Woman's Journal*, Boston, 11 Sept. 1897, 2. Copy in PAC K.B.C. Papers, Vol. 3, File 1.
7. Kit, "Goodbye Bohemia," in *Saturday Night*, 8 February 1890, 6.
8. PAC K.B.C. Papers, Vol. 2, File 40, genealogy and covering letter from Robin Rowland.
9. Ibid., Vol. 1, File 2. Her real birth date was 20 February 1856; her adopted birth date was 16 May 1864. Ibid., Vol. 2, File 40, genealogy, and Ibid., File 4, various newspaper obituaries.
10. The Blakes were one of the prominent families of Galway. Kit's response to "M.T.C.," *Mail and Empire*, 18 January 1900, 21; response to "Nan," Ibid., 5 February 1910, 21.
11. Ted Ferguson, *Kit Coleman: Queen of Hearts* (Toronto: Doubleday 1978).
12. Carol Ascher, Louise A. Di Salvo and Sara Reddick (eds.), *Between Women* (Boston: Beacon Press 1984).
13. Robin Rowland, "Kit Watkins: World's First Accredited Woman War Correspondent" in *Content*, May 1978, pp. 13-20, reprinted in B. Zwicker and D. MacDonald (eds.), *The News: Inside the Canadian Media* (Ottawa: Deneau 1982), pp. 112-120.
14. Barbara M. Freeman, "'An Impertinent Fly': Canadian Journalist Kathleen Blake Watkins Covers the Spanish-American War" in *Journalism History*, 15:4, Summer 1989.

15. Catherine L. Covert, "Journalism History and Women's Experience: A Problem in Conceptual Change," in *Journalism History* 8:1, Spring 1981, 4.
16. See, for example, Susan J. Henry, "Changing Media History Through Women's History," in Pamela J. Creedon (ed.), *Women in Mass Communication: Challenging Gender Values* (Sage Publications, Focus Editions, Vol. 106, Summer 1989).
17. See the comparison between American journalists Rheta Childe Dorr and Bessie Beatty in Zena Beth McGlashan, "Women Witness the Russian Revolution: Analyzing Ways of Seeing," in *Journalism History* 12:2, Summer 1985.
18. PAC K.B.C. Papers, Vol. 2, File 40, genealogy and covering letter from Robin Rowland. See also Rowland, "Kit's Secret," in *Content* Nov. 1978, pp. 30-31 and Dorothy Turcotte, "Kit Coleman—A Gutsy Female—Pioneer Journalist," in *Early Canadian Life*, Vol. 3, No. 4. May 1979.
19. Various sources include Emily Weaver, "Pioneer Canadian Women—'Kit' the Journalist," in *Canadian Magazine*, Vol. 49, No. 4. August 1917; Mabel Burkholder, *"Kit": Pioneer Canadian Newspaperwoman* (Hamilton Women's Press Club 1933).
20. Ferguson, *Kit Coleman.*
21. For example, *Daily Mail*, 6 Jan. 1894, 5. Kit claimed that she kept a diary. Ibid., 30 Dec. 1893, 5.
22. PAC K.B.C. Papers, Vol. 1, File 4.
23. Ibid.
24. Ibid., Vol. 2, Files 8-21.
25. For example, PAC John Willison Papers, MG 30 D29, Vol. 9, Folder 73.
26. W.J. Fitz-patrick, F.S.A., *The Life of the Very Reverend Thomas N. Burke* (London: Kegan Paul, Trench and Co., 1885). See also J.A. Rochford (ed.), *Father Burke's Sermons and Lectures* (New York: P.J. Kennedy, Excelsior Catholic Publishing House 1905).
27. Gartshore-Waterous interview.
28. Response to "Cynthia," *Daily Mail* 28 Feb. 1891, 5; *Mail and Empire*, 11 July 1896, 24; Ibid., 1 June 1895, 5.
29. Elaine Showalter, "Feminist Criticism in the Wilderness," in Elizabeth Abel (ed.), *Writing and Sexual Difference* (The University of Chicago Press 1982), 187.
30. Tillie Olsen, *Silences* (New York: Laurel Edition, Dell Publishing Co. Inc. 1983), pp. 271-277.
31. *Daily Mail*, 16 Nov. 1889, 5.
32. Paul Rutherford, *A Victorian Authority—The Daily Press in Late Nineteenth Century Canada* (Toronto: University of Toronto Press

1982), 128; Michael Schudson, *Discovering the News—A Social History of American Newspapers* (New York: Basic Books, Inc. 1978), pp. 69-74.

33. Ellen Moers, *Literary Women* (New York: Doubleday and Company 1976), pp. 122-126; 214-215.

34. Clara Thomas, "Introduction", in Catherine Parr Traill, *The Backwoods of Canada* (Toronto: McClelland and Stewart 1984), pp. 7-13. See also Carl F. Klink, "Introduction," in Susanna Moodie, *Roughing It in the Bush* (Toronto: McClelland and Stewart 1983), pp. ix-xiv.

35. Ruth Compton Brouwer, "The Between-Age Christianity of Agnes Maule Machar," in *Canadian Historical Review*, Vol. LXV, No. 3, Sept. 1984.

36. Rutherford, *A Victorian Authority*, pp. 24-35.

37. Technological and editorial changes in Canada's nineteenth century newspapers are examined by Rutherford, *A Victorian Authority* and W.H. Kesterton, *The History of Journalism in Canada* (Toronto: MacMillan of Canada. Carleton University Library Series No. 36, 1978). See also the *Mail and Empire's* 24th anniversary supplement, 24 Mar. 1896, pp. 1-4.

38. In 1891, there were 756 journalists in Canada, of whom 35 were women. Eighteen of those women worked in Ontario. Census of Canada 1891, Vol. II. (Ottawa: Queen's Printer 1893), 189. By 1900, there were over 2,000 women journalists in the United States—still only seven per cent of the total. Marion Marzolf, *Up From the Footnote* (New York: Hastings House 1978), 26.

39. Rutherford, *A Victorian Authority*, pp. 156-178.

40. A lively debate on suitable women's page material was aired in the pages of the *New York Herald*, 7 and 14 June 1891, pp. 9; Ibid., 21 and 28 June 1891, pp. 24.

41. Marjory Lang, "Separate Entrances: The First Generation of Canadian Women Journalists," in Lorraine McMullen (ed.), *Re(Dis)covering Our Foremothers: Nineteenth Century Canadian Women Writers* (Ottawa: University of Ottawa Press 1989); see also Barbara Freeman "'Every Stroke Upward': Women Journalists in Canada 1880-1906", in *Canadian Women's Studies*, Vol. 7, No. 3, (Fall 1986), reprinted in Laurence Steven, Douglas Parker and Jack Lewis (eds.), *From Reading to Writing: A Reader, Rhetoric and Handbook* (Toronto: Prentice Hall Canada 1988).

42. Response to "Romona," *Daily Mail*, 17 Sept. 1892, 8.

43. Kesterton, *A History of Journalism in Canada*, pp. 146-147; Rutherford, *A Victorian Authority*, 132.

44. Rutherford, Ibid., 132.

45. For example, Rowland, "Kit Watkins," 113.

46. Twenty-five per cent of the early women's movement activists in Canada were journalists and writers, the largest identifiable group. Carol Lee Bacchi, *Liberation Deferred? The Ideas of the English-Canadian Suffragists 1897-1918* (Toronto: University of Toronto Press 1983), 6.
47. Rutherford, *A Victorian Authority*, Appendix, pp. 235-240.
48. PAC John Willison Papers, Vol. 9, Folder 73. Letter from Kathleen Blake Coleman to John Willison, dated 1 December 1902.
49. *Daily Mail*, 9 April 1892, 5.
50. Rutherford, *A Victorian Authority*, 131.
51. Wayne Roberts, "Rocking the Cradle for the World: the New Woman and Maternal Feminism, Toronto 1877-1914," in L. Kealey (ed.), *A Not Unreasonable Claim* (Toronto: Women's Educational Press 1979) pp. 37-38.
52. Response to "Mrs. Malaprop," *Daily Mail*, 15 Dec. 1894, 5.
53. Ibid., 9 Sept. 1893, 5.
54. Response to "Laboris," Ibid., 26 Sept. 1891, 11.
55. PAC Media Club of Canada Papers, MG 28 I 232, Vol. 2, Charter Members' File, Effie Storer's Mss.
56. It is the higher estimate of J.V. MacAree, one of her colleagues on the *Mail and Empire*, who wrote that twenty dollars a week was more likely. MacAree, *The Fourth Column*, 296.
57. Jean Bannerman, *Leading Ladies* (Galt, Ont: Highland Press, 1967 rev. Dundas Ont. Carrswood 1977), 384. She cites no reference but, according to Ishbel Ross, a contemporary of Kit's, in the early 1900s the regular pay of women journalists in New York, based on word-age, was a "miserable" thirty-five to thirty-seven dollars a week. Cited in Marzolf, 40.
58. One frantic month, Kit judged 1,500 entries to a women's ad writing contest the *Daily Mail* sponsored with its advertisers in addition to her regular work. *Daily Mail*, 22 Nov. 1890, 5. She mentioned advertisers' shops and products from time to time, but insisted she did not get paid extra for her endorsements. Ibid., 30 July 1892, 5.
59. Her short stories tended to be maudlin. See, for example, "Holy Santa Claus," *Canadian Magazine*, Dec. 1898, pp. 157-159. Editors paid freelancers space rates; that is, by wordage. Marzolf, 40. By the late 1890s, Kit was complaining that syndication editors were paying male journalists ten dollars for political columns and women two dollars for fashion columns. *Mail and Empire*, 3 June 1899, 16.
60. Response to "Romona," *Daily Mail*, 6 Aug. 1892, 8.
61. Response to "York," *Mail and Empire*, 10 May 1902, pp. 18-19.
62. *Daily Mail*, 14 Feb. 1891, 5; *Mail and Empire*, 29 Oct. 1898, Part 2, 5; response to "Isabel," Ibid., 29 Nov. 1902, 18.

63. For example, Carroll Smith-Rosenberg, *Disorderly Conduct: Visions of Gender in Victorian America* (New York: Alfred A. Knopf 1985), pp. 197-215. See also Olsen, pp. 225-250.
64. See, for example, the *Mail and Empire*, 13 July 1909, 20.
65. Smith-Rosenberg, pp. 43-44.

CHAPTER 1
"WHICH IS KIT?"

> Yankee Girl (Chicago) says "...when I read your answers to
> correspondents I think you are an old lady, single, then again
> that you are married and have a large family, you have a
> motherly sort of way with you sometimes. Again that you
> are a young girl—and, Kit, I sometimes tremble lest you be
> a man. Now which are you anyway?" Asked with Yankee
> directness, answered with Irish adaptability. "Whichever you
> like best, my dear."[1]

The above response to "Yankee Girl" was typical during
Kathleen's early career when she was apparently trying to
decide just who "Kit" really was. Her real origins, which
she kept private, were far more interesting than what she
invented for a newspaper audience. Even so, Kit, with her
androgynous and maternal qualities, was fascinating
enough to draw a substantial newspaper audience.

The journalist was fond of telling her readers that she was
primarily and proudly one of the "Celtic" peoples she
described, in looking back on her career years later, as having "...more than our share of such qualities as melancholy,
humour, passion and imagination,"[2] qualities she brought
to her writing. She was the feisty Irish heroine of a tomboy
girlhood, the sensitive product of a privileged upbringing,
at once an adventurer and a lady.

The way in which she described her girlhood adventures,
her interest in topics generally considered outside of
"women's sphere," such as politics and religion, coupled

with her forceful writing style, led to humorous exchanges with curious readers, who were convinced at first that she actually was a man. Her identity was further confused when she dispensed practical, motherly advice or discussed household matters, etiquette, proper ladylike behaviour and child-rearing and lent her support to charitable causes such as fresh air funds for poor children. Kit's maternal side was warm, sympathetic and, when the occasion demanded, sternly conventional.

"Woman's Kingdom" grew quickly, evolving in two years from a column into an attractive feature of one or more pages, with pen and ink illustrations, an editorial, a number of short paragraphs on topical items under the heading "Pot-pourri," some poetry and the "Correspondence" section in which Kit answered inquiries from people who usually wrote to her under pen-names.[3] In a separate section, "Our Letter Club," she involved her readers in debates on topics ranging from the serious to the silly and often presented her own point of view. Politics, economics, religion, race, and various social and moral issues as well as "light" romantic topics generally relegated to "women's sphere" were all discussed.[4] Her audience comprised not only regular readers of the *Daily Mail*, but also subscribers to the *Weekly Mail* across Canada and in other countries.

Veracity was not one of Kit's strong points. Her fanciful way of writing—especially about her childhood and adolescent adventures—was not lost on her readers, some of whom wrote to accuse her of invention. Her own measure of truth in her writing is revealing: "LITTLE COUNTRY MAIDEN... The incident you mention was merely taken from big Old London and transposed to Toronto. It is taken from real life, therefore true."[5]

Literary license served to both disguise and reveal incidents in Kathleen's own life. She never told her personal story directly in print, but there are many allusions to it, often in the third person, in her columns and fiction manuscripts. The following account of her private life is taken mostly from genealogical records,[6] her uncle-priest's biography[7] and family lore.[8]

Kathleen Blake Coleman was not a daughter of the prominent Blake family of Galway, as Kit claimed.[9] Her father, Patrick Ferguson, came from the village of Castleblakeney, in the west of Ireland. He was an Irish landlord with modest holdings and little money. Her mother was Mary Burke of Galway, the daughter of a baker. There was one other child, an older daughter, Margaret. The mother was the sister of a prominent Dominican priest, Father Thomas Burke, a man known for his strong social conscience. His statue still stands overlooking the area known as the Claddagh, the traditional fishing and working class area of Galway. Father Burke was one of his niece Kathleen's fondest mentors and, it appears, one of her early role-models. Biographical sources and her own writing indicate that the people who had most influence on both Kathleen and Kit were males, which helps to explain her androgynous and conflicted public identity.

She was educated at Loretto Abbey, a Roman Catholic boarding school at Rathfarnham, near Tallagh, where Father Burke was the spiritual advisor to the nuns. At some point in her adolescence, she was sent to finishing school in Belgium. There she was exposed to a much freer world than was allowed her in Ireland, where the Roman Catholic Church was a strong and repressive force. According to her grandchildren, the independent-minded young woman left the Church because of that repression and particularly because it had a condemned list of books the faithful were forbidden to read. Her insistence on freedom of speech, of the press and of religion were constant themes in her later writing as a journalist.

Her rejection of the Church may also have had something to do with what appears to have been a very unconventional love life. It is not clear if all of her three marriages were legal. Kathleen's first husband, whom she married when she was twenty years old, was an Irish merchant, Thomas Willis of Holymount, a middle-aged man who was quite well off.[10]

19

According to her grandchildren, it was not a happy union and when her husband died, apparently after a drunken fall from a horse, Kathleen was left penniless.[11] Her father-in-law had stipulated, in his own will, that if his son died without a male heir, the family fortune was to revert to his widowed daughter, not his daughter-in-law. She was forced to make her own living.

Kathleen got influential acquaintances to write letters of reference recommending her as a governess or companion. One was signed by the Archbishop of Dublin, who mentioned that she was a niece of Father Burke. Another was from Winifred M. Wyse, a close friend of the priest,[12] who suggested that Kathleen's husband "having lost all his fortune and being obliged in consequence to go to America" left her behind to support herself. Since there is a record of her marriage, but none of her husband's death, it is possible that he emigrated. But records from that period are often incomplete. Kathleen or Mrs. Wyse might have found it better that she be represented as a married woman, rather than the attractive young widow she was, in order to better her chances of employment. To help her in her quest, Mrs. Wyse wrote of Kathleen:

> She has a sweet temper, is obliging, bright and clever and very fond of children...a good Musician, speaks French with a pure accent, and is well acquainted with English literature in fact has had an excellent education. ...Mrs. Willis is also well known to the Dowager Marchioness of Londonderry and Lady Herbert of Lea.[13]

Kathleen emigrated to Canada,[14] where she met and married Edward J. Watkins and gave birth to their son and daughter.[15] Their grandchildren believe that the charming Watkins was the love of her life, but the couple had a dreadful time making ends meet. They moved from Toronto to Winnipeg, where he worked as a commercial traveller and she taught French and music. At one point she was forced to sell the fur coat that kept her warm during the bitterly cold Northwest winter in order to pay the bills.[16]

Kathleen's second husband, E.J. Watkins 1880s.
(Bryne & Co/National Archives of Canada/PA-172133)

The couple moved back to Toronto[17] and eventually separated when it became clear to Kathleen that her hard-
drinking husband was a philanderer. He may have been a
bigamist, as well. He apparently told her, when she threatened to divorce him, that she couldn't because they weren't
really married to begin with. He already had a wife in
England. If that was true, it meant that the children were
"illegitimate," a scandalous state of affairs in her day.[18]

Although Kathleen never wrote her own story directly,
she left several hints of her unhappiness. On the back of
Watkins' photograph, she wrote "Sic Transit Gloria—
Amor"[19] and there are numerous references in her fiction
to doomed marriages and love affairs. The short stories are
often about alcoholic and/or philandering men and the
women who loved them and are set in various cities, including London, Winnipeg and New York.[20]

It apparently took Kathleen years to get over the break
up, but her most pressing concern was her children, with
whom she was very close. Her son, nicknamed "Thady" or
"Teddie," was about five years old in 1890, and probably
went to kindergarten.[21] He apparently lived with his father,
not always happily. Once, when he was eight, he walked
half-way across Toronto alone to persuade his mother to let
him live with her.[22] Later, in a letter postmarked "Parkdale"
and addressed to her at the *Mail* office, he promised to see
her soon and bring his mending. It reads in part:

> You dear old mother. I know your (sic) lonely and so am I.
> O! so much. I will come down as soon as I can and see you.
> Letters are no good they are only dreams…Your photograph
> looks at me and I kiss it every morning, noon and night and
> now you dear Brer Rabbit give me one big kiss X now and
> as it is nearly bed time I will say good-by (sic).[23]

The daughter, also Kathleen but nicknamed "Patsy,"
was, as an adult, quite reticent about the family's private
life, even with her own children.[24] But her notes in her
mother's papers refer to a split in the Watkins domicile
between Parkdale and rooms downtown and hints about
different life styles. It appears that her mother took her to

the nuns at a Roman Catholic boarding school where she remained for some years.[25] The likely choice was Loretto Abbey in Toronto. It was run by the sisters of the Institute of the Blessed Virgin Mary, the same order that ran the Loretto Abbey Kathleen senior attended in Ireland. The Toronto convent records are incomplete but, between 1896 and 1898, there were several students there by the name of Watkins, including a "Kathleen."[26]

It is not known whether or not Edward Watkins helped support the children financially, but, either before or after their marriage broke up, his wife went to work as a journalist. She may have started on a weekly newspaper as the writer of a column on graphology—the interpretation of character based on a person's handwriting[27]—and later mentioned having served an unpaid apprenticeship for about a year.[28] But it is certain that, during August 1890, she sold several freelance articles, signed Kit, to Edmund Sheppard, the editor of a Canadian weekly magazine, *Saturday Night*.

Sheppard had learned the hard way to recognize and encourage talented women journalists. Some years earlier, he had refused to hire another struggling writer, Sara Jeannette Duncan, on the specious grounds that the last woman on his staff did not work out. Duncan went on to become a successful journalist and novelist, prompting Sheppard to change his attitude toward newspaperwomen. His proteges included Kit and one of her better-known contemporaries, Elmira Elliott Atkinson ("Madge Merton").[29]

According to Kathleen's personal papers, her first published article was a romantic piece, set in Toronto, called "The Old Organ Grinder," whose music brought the writer back to a sunny day in Venice.[30] She quickly followed with other articles, including a vivid historical essay on the French Revolution and an Irish ghost story, narrated by a male, about a doctor's encounter with a banshee.[31] The articles were representative of the kind of writing she became famous for later: they were descriptive, knowledgeable and romantic.

At the end of October, 1889, her Kit byline appeared for the first time in the *Daily Mail's* Saturday women's feature, "Woman's Kingdom."[32] She had approached the newspaper's editor-in-chief, Edward Farrer, with "...a little theory of her own concerning Adam and Eve in the Garden of Eden, which, it need hardly be explained, was a distinct departure from the accepted scriptural version."[33] Farrer, then in his thirties, was "a brilliant, amiable, humorous, mysterious, ironic..." Irishman who was an influential force at the *Mail*.[34] He liked the article and hired her.

Despite its insistence on political independence, the *Mail* was still identified with the Conservatives and many of its readers were middle-class, party supporters. Kathleen's first job was to establish an identity with which her readers would feel comfortable. In the beginning of her career at the *Mail*, she relied greatly on her Irish background to develop her persona and entertain her audience.

She hinted at her origins at first, often describing an unnamed family of Irish girls who lived in "a great, big, rambling country house on the other side of the water," with their affectionate mother and a somewhat stern father.[35] They were not very well off, but the "gentleman farmer" of the family would insist that his daughters dress for dinner:

> Semi-toilette, perhaps, with just a little bit of the throat showing, and elbow sleeves; and the mater would "fix up," too, and the finger bowls were there, and the little Russian glasses for holding tiny bouquets, and the snowy Irish linen and the old man servant who was almost one of the family, whose name was Micky, and the dinner might be shabby and uneven, with wretched soup maigre to begin with and fine Irish salmon to follow, and so on, good and bad in layers, like most Irish affairs, while Micky would pour the thin St. Julien into the big green glasses and look as proud of the "fambly" as though he was filling out Mumm's Dry or Moet en Chandon, and everyone was shabbily grand and kept up appearances in a correct manner on, I would be afraid to tell you how little a year.[36]

24

Almost a year after she started at the *Mail*, Kit was staring out her window, day-dreaming to her readers about the Irish family again, when she mused "I leave ....why shouldn't I say it—my old Irish home, which for the moment is just outside my window." At that point, an older female companion, "Theodocia," who is reading over her shoulder, scolds her for her "untruth...I mean, blarnyfied" copy, but the journalist ignores her.[37]

Kit's childhood was a privileged one by most Irish standards. She claimed to be a descendant of a deposed Irish king whom she called Brian MacMurrough, King of Connaught.[38] The household had a number of servants: they included Micky the manservant and "Betty" the cook, a comical, pipe-smoking old woman who appeared in many of Kit's columns and short stories.[39]

Kit's childhood home was familiar territory to the real-life Kathleen, although it is not clear exactly whose home it really was. According to her daughter Patsy Gartshore's notes, it was based on a house called Creevaghmore, where her mother grew up. Official genealogical information, however, states that the family of Thomas Willis, Kathleen's first husband, owned a house at "Creevagh." Since they were well off, the house and grounds she depicted may have been theirs, but the relatively impoverished circumstances may have been those experienced by her own family.

One of the strongest influences in Kit's life was her father, who, she wrote in a revealing anecdote, had been furious when she was born, since he had no son:

> I must here admit, however, that when my unfortunate self
> was born my father was so angry with me for being a poor
> little woman child, and, what was worse, he was so angry
> with my mother that he left the house accompanied by an
> old servant man ...and painted a certain Irish town a bright
> and vivid green—he was too much of an Irishman to paint
> it red—and neither master nor man turned up for a week,
> and, mother used to say, there was peace and quietness, for
> a while, at least, in that old Irish house, filled with girls as
> it was.[40]

The same story is repeated in Kathleen's unpublished Irish novel in which father and daughter grow to understand each other and form a close relationship. "Bob Travers" is a proud, stern man and his daughter "Cauth" is a "wild one...a devileen" who accompanies him, hand-in-hand, on the depressing rounds of his failing farm.[41]

To her newspaper readers, Kit described her young self, not as a Victorian, ladylike little "sunbeam," but an active, mischievous little girl, closer to the "hoyden," but without the latter's more negative characteristics. In her own mind, she took on the role of a son. She became "...the boy of the house myself in the old days, and did all those things I ought not to have done."[42] She loved to romp and run and learned to handle horses so that she could ride to hounds— sidesaddle as was proper for women—when she was older. Her father, who taught her many things, introduced her to riding by threatening to thrash her if she showed any fright the first time she mounted a horse.[43]

The portrait of her father fit the literary conventions of the time. In Victorian literature, "masculine strength and sound morality " were typical virtues of the patriarch of a happy home, but paternal masculinity could also be depicted as "cold and barren." Fathers saw themselves as responsible for various aspects of their daughters' education, including some schooling, which many fictional Victorian girls received in "papa's study."[44]

For all his sternness, Kit's father was a liberal and cultured man who instilled in her a life-long love of books, especially those of Charles Dickens, and taught her about science, nature and wildlife.[45] He tried to limit her to works considered suitable for young women, but later gave her free access to the family library. In other versions of the story, she related how she hid books he did not approve of her reading, such as *Jane Eyre*, in the potato dike in the family garden to read later in secret.[46]

Some aspects of Kit's father's character may have been borrowed from Kathleen's real-life uncle, Father Thomas Burke, who was a famous preacher. For example, at different times, Kit credited both her uncle and her father for giving her the pet-name that became her nom-de-plume. Kit, which could have been short for either Kathleen or Christopher, evolved from "(my) supposed likeness to Christopher Columbus," a reference to her adventuresome spirit.[47] She wrote that it came from a clergyman "orator" close to her heart, an account supported by Father Burke's biographer.[48] But she later contradicted herself, saying it came from her father.[49]

What is clear is Kathleen's devotion to her uncle. Father Burke's biographer paints him as a kind, humorous man with a strong intellect and outstanding oratorical abilities. Privately, he was self-deprecating, shy and melancholic and was often depressed because of a chronic stomach ailment.[50] He was fond of Dickens, art and music and loved to put on comedies and plays with his young niece for the entertainment of family and friends.[51] As a priest, he counselled his flock to be tolerant of each others' religious differences and charitable to all,[52] themes Kit later took up in her journalism. When he died, Kathleen was so distraught that, forsaking any pretense of "feminine" behaviour, she forced her way through the large funeral crowd to the head of the casket, where she insisted on taking the place of one of the pallbearers.[53] Later, Kit wrote that when a man she loved above all others, an unnamed preacher and "orator," died she was so upset that, for awhile, she lost her faith in God.[54]

The public Kit was much closer to her father/uncle than she was to her mother, who fit the stereotype of Victorian literature as the "moral, spiritual and practical guide" of the family.[55] Kit depicted her as an "adoring wife and mother," the soul of meekness and gentleness.[56] She was an accomplished musician who taught her daughters how to play several instruments, an indication of great inner strength, considering that she was blind. She bore her disability with much fortitude[57] and would often admonish the young Kit with advice designed to teach her to be selfless and charitable, conditions of the contemporary ideal of "femininity."[58] One day the adult journalist found, at the bottom of her trunk, a lap desk full of letters:

> ...old, old mother-letters, where we read that "somebody" must learn to be sweet and kind, to love all things, for all were made by God, that even a wretched, hunted fox, or tiny field-mouse is "God's little beast."[59]

The letters were sent to her when she was a child in boarding school. Kit never referred to Loretto Abbey, but claimed she was enrolled in a school in Dublin at the age of six, where she was subjected to a thorough, but uneven, education in the classics.[60]

As Kit wrote more about the Irish family, the houseful of girls became the home of just two sisters, the writer and the older one, "Margaret," a talented violinist who grew up to marry a local farmer. The journalist would tell her readers how the pair, who were very close, liked to play pranks[61] and delighted in riding pell-mell over the Irish countryside, displaying a total lack of ladylike decorum.[62]

Kit never ignored an opportunity to mention her riding prowess. In one episode, set during the Irish troubles of the early 1880s, vandals secretly cut her stirrup strap, but she skillfully managed to keep her seat when she unwittingly galloped her horse.[63] She often mentioned riding to hounds, and remembered two of her mounts with great fondness—Trina and King Rufus. Both horses were hard for any woman to handle during the excitement of a fox hunt—unless she was Kit: "Thank Goodness no lady ever rode King Rufus but me and I won three brushes with him, which is a big thing when you hunt as we hunt in Ireland."[64]

Her descriptions of her own strength and agility as a horsewoman—coupled with her choice of pen-name—led to a debate in her pages about her real gender. One Saturday, just a few months after she started on the *Mail*, she wrote about riding to hounds on Trina, who stubbornly refused to jump water. The only time she ever swore, she admitted, was when she was trying to handle the balky horse.[65] Judging from Kit's comments, readers began to surmise that, since ladies didn't swear, she must be a man. Under the sarcastic heading "A Sharp Girl," she quoted a letter that she claimed she received from "A Would-be Mrs. 'Kit'":

> "In the first place a woman taking the nom de plume Kit would certainly have chosen le plus doux nom of Kitty; also in describing the hunt in Ireland (which I enjoyed very much) she would have had no difficulty in finding epithets by which to express her indignation, such as, you nasty horrid beast, you contrary animal, etc., etc., and would have felt that she would have had une grande satisfaction."

Kit replied, with some spirit, that after her sketch about the hunt had appeared, she had received a number of letters accusing her of being male:

> How sorry I am that I ever took upon myself to describe that hunt in Ireland! ... (The writer) infers from my masculine language that I am a man. I feel more like a fox with the hounds after him in full cry. As to satisfaction, all I can say is that I had a good deal more satisfaction in using the forcible language I did than I would have had in calling my horse "a nasty horrid beast." That may be more womanlike and ladylike, and proper, but one doesn't feel very proper and ladylike when one has a sulky, bucking brute of a mare to manage. [66]

The exchange started a debate about Kit's real identity that lasted the better part of three years. The journalist always insisted that her correspondence was real[67] and never admitted making up "A Would-Be Mrs. 'Kit's'" letter to stir up her readers. She played quite a game with them about her gender: she would flirt with correspondents of both sexes, tease them, become indignant at their inquisitiveness and throw in red herrings to keep the guessing game going.[68] At one point, she wrote that, although she wasn't really a man, she often wished she was. She envied men because of their relative freedom and privileges and the attention they received from most women.[69] Her vision was upper middle class and her tone sometimes humorous. "I shall long—as I often do, to be a man and rejoice in my pipe,

"Which is Kit?"
The *Mail's* illustrator has fun with Kit's identity, 1890.

my yacht, my club and—but I mustn't say naughty things..."[70]

Her readers seemed quite engaged by the discussion. "Othello" testified to the androgynous way in which she represented herself, concluded she was really a man, and wondered what she looked like: "You ape the affectations of a woman, I must say, extremely well, but your virile thoughts break out sometimes and betray that you are a lord of creation." Kit's response was to have the *Daily Mail's* illustrator produce sketches of eight very different looking individuals—four women and four men—which were published in the same column in which "Othello's" letter appeared, under the heading: "Which is Kit?"[71]

The guessing games served an important purpose—to protect Kathleen's privacy. Her curious readers wanted to know everything about her, including her age and marital circumstances, but she was not about to tell them that she was thirty-four years old, separated from a man who may have been a bigamist and supporting their two children. Kit refused to answer any letters privately or meet her readers in person, explaining to them that she was afraid some of their more romantic illusions of her would be shattered.[72] In real life, she assured one correspondent, she was:

> ...a very plain, middle-aged woman..Plain brown eyes, not deep or long-lashed, brown hair slightly mixed with grey; nondescript sort of nose, wide mouth, with tired lines at the corners, average complexion, rather red; average figure, ugly hands and feet. There! How do you like the picture! You would have it, you know.[73]

She invented a "personal life" for Kit, who lived in a house with her older friend "Theodocia," a wise, stern and occasionally comical woman who sometimes acted as the journalist's conscience and guide. Kit later told her readers that the "Theodocia" character was based on "a dear, comfortable, delicious woman friend" but would not name her.[74] Both were "toddling old bodies not much interested in babies' things."[75]

31

Readers of the "Kingdom" were not convinced. Many, like "Johnny Jump-Up," thought "Theodocia" must represent Kit's husband in real life.[76] Rather than explain her personal circumstances, the journalist used the older woman character to help her deflect intrusive questions with humour. In one of her columns, she related a conversation between three women which, she claimed, she and "Theodocia" overheard in the street.

> "Is she married?"
> "Who, Kit?"
> "Oh yes, to an awful pudgy little man I hear. I believe it's he does all the work and she gets the credit for it."[77]

Kit had been particularly reticent about her real-life children, but late in 1890, she began to use her experiences with an unnamed boy and baby girl to entertain her readers or illustrate a child-rearing point, such as the inadvisability of corporal punishment, especially for girls.[78] She also introduced a short-lived feature in "Woman's Kingdom" called "Children's Chats" for which readers were invited to send in their offsprings' cute sayings.[79] She contributed some herself but did not, at first, identify the children she wrote about as her own—she was their "Auntie," rather than their "mother."[80] She would sometimes discuss domestic doings in her own "private life"—such as her efforts to get out her column amid the chaos of spring cleaning[81]—but did not talk about her child care arrangements.

Even though Kathleen created a maternal side for Kit, there were still readers who persisted in thinking that the journalist was a man. It was partly because she did not shy away from discussing current political or social concerns or events, or expressing her opinion on intellectual and scientific topics, unless she thought the subject would be too complex or boring for most readers.[82] Although she did not identify herself as a feminist, she insisted on being accepted as an intelligent woman writer: "We all have a right to express our opinions. I do so, though I am only a woman."[83]

She was particularly outspoken about Irish politics and was a passionate advocate of Home Rule. In late 1890, the English Liberal leader, W.E. Gladstone, who supported Home Rule, disassociated himself from the Irish Party leader Charles Stewart Parnell, purportedly because of the latter's adulterous affair with Kitty O'Shea. Their political differences went much deeper than that, however. Several Irish politicians—Tim Healy, Justin McCarthy, John Dillon, William O'Brien and others—subsequently tried to take over the Irish Party from Parnell.[84] Kit had more faith in Gladstone than any of the Irish politicians, whom she blamed for the mess. She was far blunter about them in print than she ever would be about Canadian politicians:

> FROM PADDY'S LAND—...You ask me my opinion on Irish affairs and want to know if I am a Parnellite. No. I'm a Gladstonian, if it will do you any good to hear that. There's one thing I'd have you know, though, and that is I am not a Healyite. I wouldn't uphold that vulgar little wretch if I was to gain Home Rule for Ireland tomorrow by it. ... McCarthy will never make a leader. Neither will Sexton, Dillon or that gas-bag O'Brien... Parnell's sin, my friend, consisted in being found out.[85]

In contrast, Kit, who once described herself as a Conservative in Canada and the "opposite in Ireland,"[86] was careful about Canadian politicians, working as she did for a maverick, but still Conservative, newspaper. She loved discussing issues, but rarely committed herself on them. As she coyly told "Wragge":

> I would much rather sit on a fence myself, with my feet tucked decorously beneath my skirts, than jump down into the mud and get wet and draggle-tailed and vilified. Wouldn't you, girls? Friend Wragge, you are up to your eyes in the fray, but you forget that the lookers-on see most of the game.[87]

When she did express an opinion, it did not always follow the lead of the *Daily Mail* itself. Up until that time, the powers-that-be at the newspaper, including the managing director, Christopher Bunting, contributor Goldwin Smith and editor Edward Farrer, were among the politicians and editorial writers who had been hotly debating the trade relationship between Canada and the United States. Smith went as far as to propose annexation of Canada to the U.S., a position also favoured by the influential but more subtle Farrer. After Farrer left the *Mail* in 1890, the easily manipulated Bunting, a former Tory MP, backed away from continentalism and sought to re-establish ties with the party.[88]

In the meantime, the liberal critics of Prime Minister John A. Macdonald's National Policy were convinced that it was benefitting large manufacturers and monopolists to the detriment of ordinary working Canadians. They demanded an end to protective tariffs on Canadian goods, which they blamed for low wages, and called for free trade with the United States instead.[89]

Kit discussed free trade with her readers in Our Letter Club, and received many replies, including one from "M" who wrote that free trade between the two countries, not annexation, was the answer. Kit agreed, but added that free trade should come gradually:

> It would never do, however, for free trade to come to us too suddenly. First of all the present tariff should be lowered so that our manufacturers would not suffer by the free trade policy. The policy of protection is suicidal.[90]

By introducing political and economic issues into her "Kingdom," however, Kit risked losing the segment of her audience that mattered most to her editors, ordinary women. With the annexation issue, for example, all the letters that arrived one week were from men, which surprised the journalist, who found it strange that they would write to a women's page: "I really thought men despised us as far as politics and the great things of life are concerned."[91]

There were many male readers of the *Daily Mail* who thought, however, that Kit was trying to be too intellectual and often, too controversial. This was particularly true when she discussed religion. One aspect of religious intolerance at the time was the long-standing bigotry and mistrust

34

between English Protestant and French Catholic, a situation the *Mail* had been milking for all its worth in its campaign for annexation with the United States. In fact, managing director Bunting was a "genuinely bigoted" anti-Catholic,[92] but this did not appear to affect what Kathleen wrote. It is quite possible that her experience of sectarian differences in Ireland influenced her, as Kit, to be non-judgmental— "the bigot is never a noble man," she told her readers[93]— and she had ongoing debates with several correspondents about the Roman Catholic church.[94]

While she would discuss religious issues in general, and often expressed Christian sentiments in her vignettes,[95] Kit learned quickly to avoid discussing the details of her own spiritual life. She once made the mistake of hinting that she did not believe in certain doctrines, such as the resurrection of all souls.[96] It might have been that column that prompted a visit to her office from a Protestant minister, who literally turned his back on her because she "didn't go to church twice on Sundays."[97] After that, she generally became annoyed when correspondents implied that she was anti-religious and told them to mind their own business.[98]

At the time, Protestant Canada was going through a religious crisis, as were Britain and the United States, over the theories of Charles Darwin, with those who favoured his scientific explanation of the evolution of humankind pitted against those who saw his theories as a challenge to the Biblical account of the creation and thereby a threat to religious belief. Like Father Burke, Kit saw no conflict between science and religion and admired Darwin.[99] But when she briefly explained Darwinism to "Perambus,"[100] she was criticized by "Darwinian," who didn't think a woman should be dealing with such topics at all. She heatedly replied:

> DARWINIAN—...Ignorance and impertinence go often hand in hand. It is thus with you... I know very little of science, I am sorry to say, but whenever a query appears which I think I am capable of answering, I object, on my doing so, to the impertinent remark, from an ignorant member of the greater(?) sex, that a woman is "ridiculous" when she writes

on a matter of which, according to my correspondent, "not
a man in ten knows anything."[101]

By this time, many newspaper writers in North America
were discussing Darwin's theories sympathetically.[102] The
debate was more than just a dispute among religious fac-
tions. The historian Ramsay Cook argues that it "led religious people to attempt to salvage Christianity by trans-
forming it into an essentially social religion,"[103] which
stressed such reforms as legal protection for street children
and havens for "fallen" women, rather than personal salvation. Other scholars see the Victorian emphasis on social
reform as an anxious response to the changes brought about
by the industrial revolution, particularly urbanization with
its attendant problems of poverty and crime. Street children,
especially those who sold newspapers, and other waifs and
strays were the focus of much of this middle-class concern,
not just because they were "ill-clad, undisciplined and, most
importantly unschooled," but because of what they did.
Begging, idleness and ignorance were seen as the begin-
nings of immorality and crime.[104]

Kit was a firm supporter of social action to help the dis-
advantaged, but felt that too many middle-class reformers
were pretentious and hypocritical in their behaviour
towards the poor and the working class. Those who wish
to help them, she wrote, should bring love, not condescen-
sion to the task.[105] There were many middle-class women
helping to run institutions for "fallen" women and female
offenders, or who were intent on keeping immigrant and
working-class girls and women out of trouble through
domestic training at industrial schools and other pro-
grams.[106] But Kit declared that there were still too many society matrons who, mindful of their own supposedly sterling
virtue, turned away in disgust from fallen "Magdalenes."[107]

She herself could be patronizing, however, particularly
towards street children. Using a romantically maternal tone,
she wrote about them often during her first few years on
the *Daily Mail*. She commended the Salvation Army, which

was often subjected to ridicule by mainstream Protestants, after she had visited its hostel for "baby toughs,"[108] while newspaper boys, under her pen, took on the romantic shadings of Dickens' Tiny Tim.[109]

Despite her purported liberalism, Kit was not entirely free of religious and racial prejudice. She considered Jews admirably businesslike but religiously unenlightened[110] and orientals dirty and an economic threat as cheap labour, especially in British Columbia where many had settled.[111] She hardly mentioned native Indians at all. When she did she tended to take a noble savage view, mourning the ruin that the white man's ways—and whiskey—had brought to the indigenous peoples.[112]

Kit was also something of a social snob. In an article about proper dress, she blithely assumed: "Many of you girls have doubtless been presented at court on one of your visits to England."[113] When readers complained that the average housewife could not afford the expensive ingredients she recommended in her recipes, she acknowledged her mistake and suggested that they send in their own for publication.[114]

Criticism was an occupational hazard of a journalist's life, particularly if she was a female who often strayed into the more intellectual "male" domain or challenged some of the *cliché* staid conventions of Victorian times. Kit was very aware of the journalistic demands of her profession, but did not always conform. Although she took to heart Christopher Bunting's instructions that she "should not write over the heads of the people,"[115] she at first eschewed the emerging journalistic "objectivity"[116] trend for "individuality" in her writing. She liked gossipy "talks" and believed her readers did, too:

> They tell you that to be a journalist you must never let your heart run away with you. What a foolish saying! You must bury yourself and your troubles and joys and pipe up to amuse the people! Nonsense. The editorial "we" is about played out.[117]

37

Her writing, as a result, was very direct and personal in style rather than cool and impartial. She appeared to accept that it was therefore inferior to the work of the male journalists and actually agreed with one reader's unfavourable comparisons of her "twaddle" with "the facts" written by her colleague, H.H. Wiltshire, who wrote a column on current topics in the *Mail* every Saturday as "The Flaneur."[118] "The Flaneur" was a particular friend of Kit's and they sometimes threw bouquets to each other in print—he dwelling on her attractiveness and womanliness as much as her journalistic skill.[119] Kathleen may have relied on Wiltshire to guide her during her first few years on the *Mail*, during which Kit learned, among other things, to take attacks from readers in stride. Where once unfair or unwarranted criticism could irritate or upset her to the point of tears,[120] she invoked the authority of an unnamed newspaperman in adopting a new attitude:

> TRINIE—...Call me a man! My dear, they call me everything—heathen, viper, tarradiddler, all sorts of unpleasant names; but I'm quite used to it by this time, and have arrived at the conclusion, backed up by a newspaper man, that abuse is a thing that rolls in by the bushel to a newspaper office, and that without it we would have no use for waste paper baskets.[121]

There were plenty of men in her profession who were not supportive, and she found their criticisms difficult to bear. Occasionally, she would receive nasty letters from male journalists too cowardly to sign their names, such as "Cosmopolitan," whose unpublished comments led her to remark: "... when it comes to reviling and so-called smart(?) sayings, it takes a male operator of the craft to do the dirty work."[122] Criticism of women journalists like herself also took the public form of editorial jokes and satire. The *Daily Mail* once declared that women reporters talked so much during interviews that they had nothing to report on afterwards[123] and Kit herself was featured in the Canadian magazine, *Grip*, in a satire of female journalists. In it, "the ornate Kitty"—a reference to her writing style—scooped, with "a little horrid, mocking laugh" another "Giddy Young Gairl" reporter, who wrote her copy on scented notepaper. [124] In her reaction to the piece, Kit wrote that she was torn between pride at being noticed and fear of *Grip* and its editor, the popular journalist-caricaturist John Wilson Bengough:

> Someone writes asking me if I "did not feel cheap" when I saw the way our esteemed contemporary *Grip* parodied some twaddle of mine. I beg to assure my sweet correspondent that I felt proud. I had a quiet, friendly chat with *Grip* himself lately.... a wise old raven before whom "the ornate Kitty" knows better than to show her claws...Kit will always hold out a friendly velvet paw to her friend the raven. "Because you're afraid of him," says calm Theodocia as she sits knitting in her corner. Well, now, there's something in that, too. Maybe I am. [125]

As far as newspaper editors in general were concerned, women's news took a definite second place to male concerns. With all her efforts to gather material and long hours writing answers to the "piles"[126] of letters she received, Kit was aware that her work had low priority at the *Mail*. Especially during political campaigns, she would find that her "Kingdom" shrank from two pages to one. She appeared impatient with the male monopoly of news space, but, at the same time, implicitly devalued her own work: "...elections and single taxes and all kinds of men-fads are going on, and the Editor will crowd us out if we don't cut our chatter short."[127]

Her main purpose, as far as her editors were concerned, was to attract a predominantly female audience, preferably by discussing domestic issues such as housekeeping and child-rearing and espousing conventional ideals of femininity and womanliness when giving guidance and advice. She devoted many essays, "Pot-pourri" paragraphs and answers to correspondents on these topics. Many of her readers particularly responded to her sympathetic answers to those who wrote to her with their problems. She was peppered with letters on, as she once put it, "politics, polemics, physiology and pimples,"[128] and was amazed by what they showed her of "the seamy sides of humanity" as well as "such humility, generosity, common sense and sympathy as would make you wonder."[129] She, in turn, was expected to provide warm, motherly advice, especially in times of trial, something she considered her duty even when she was accused of being sentimental in her responses:

> NORMA writes a pleasant natural letter, a sympathizing little note in which she says something that is a testimony to the use of this correspondence column. "On lonely days," writes Norma, "looking for help and encouragement, I always find, in Saturday's MAIL some reply that speaks to my heart exactly as if written to me, and that I alone was the one spoken to, I only the chief sufferer in this world of sufferers, and so dear Kit I must thank you and tell you that you have helped me to know the uses of adversity, and the dignity of suffering, as well as how to be strong." And that is just what we want to do in this column, Norma, to answer questions truly as well as lies in one's power; to touch some one suffering heart, and relieve it of the too great burden of human sorrow. One may be romantic and silly and sentimental, but though people may laugh at "sentiment," the world would be a poor place without it. A woman without a touch of some kind of sentiment is an uninteresting creature, but, thank God, I have not met many mothers who, common-place, practical, hard, as they may be in other walks of life, are not without "sentiment" where the babies are concerned.[130]

The maternal aspect of the Kit persona was her saving grace in that it blunted the edge of her more forthright characteristics and helped to allay criticism of her as a woman writer. To be a success in journalism, it was necessary for her to attract and hold an audience without threatening their perceptions of women's proper role.

As a hard-working journalist and sole supporter of two children, Kathleen might well be expected to have considered all aspects of women's condition and the political, economic and social reforms that would have improved it. Among current ideas were those of equal pay for equal work and suffrage. But, reluctant to be labelled as a "new woman" or worse, a "masculine, platform" woman, she learned very quickly just how far Kit could go in espousing women's rights.

Notes

1. *Daily Mail*, 30 May 1891, 11.
2. Vancouver *News Advertiser*, 3 May 1914, 10.
3. As a rule, she did not print the actual letters from her correspondents "because to do so would in many cases give offence, and cause serious injury." *Mail and Empire*, 10 July 1909, 16.
4. In Kathleen's private papers, there are scrapbooks containing newspaper clippings from the 1870s to the 1890s, reflecting an interest in everything from various disasters to spiritualism. It is not clear, however, that they were hers. PAC K.B.C. Papers. Vol. 1, Files 11 and 12.
5. *Daily Mail*, 10 Jan. 1891, 9.
6. PAC K.B.C. Papers, Vol. 2, File 40, genealogy and covering letter to Robin Rowland. Ibid., Vol. 3, File 4, courtship letter from Patrick Ferguson to Mary Burke, dated Castleblakeney, 28 November 1852.
7. Fitz-patrick, *The Life of the Very Reverend Thomas N. Burke*; J. Rochford (ed.), *Father Burke's Sermons and Lectures*.
8. Gartshore-Waterous interview.
9. She claimed she "kept" the name to honour her father. *Mail and Empire*, 20 Dec. 1902, 21. No connection with either of her parents has come to light. She also used the Blake surname for some of her short story characters. See, for example, Kathleen Blake Watkins, "The Secret Meeting and What Came Of It," PAC K.B.C. Papers, Vol. 2, File 23.
10. Such arranged marriages were common in Ireland at the time. Lee in *Women in Irish History*, 38. Kit later claimed she was married at sixteen. Response to "Avon," *Mail and Empire*, 14 Mar. 1896, 6.
11. Kit once intimated to a reader that she did not love her first husband and the marriage had been unhappy. Response to "Dick," Ibid., 17 Nov. 1900, 16.
12. Fitz-patrick, Vol. 1, 336.
13. Both the Archbishop's and Mrs. Wyse's letters are in PAC K.B.C. Papers, Vol. 1, File 2.
14. Kit wrote that she travelled extensively before emigrating to Canada and that she had lived in Chicago for a year. *Daily Mail*, 20 Dec. 1890, 5; response to "Richard Carstone," 3 Sept. 1892, 6.
15. The children's ages are not clear. In later columns, Kit indicated that her son was born on 28 July 1885 and her daughter was born 4 October 1887. *Mail and Empire*, 29 July 1899, 14; response to "Maud", Ibid., 23 Mar. 1901, 17; response to "Elizabeth", Ibid., 19 Oct. 1901, 18. The granddaughter, Kit Waterous, is not sure about her uncle's birth date, but says he was two years older than her mother whose

birth date she gives as 4 Oct. 1889, not 1887. Telephone conversation with Barbara M. Freeman 21 Aug. 1989.

16. Gartshore-Waterous Interview. E.J. Watkins, commercial traveller, is listed in the 1888 N.W. Ontario, Manitoba and N.W. Territories Directory and Gazetteer as a resident of Winnipeg. Kit referred to living in the Northwest on several occasions. See, for example, her response to "Jack," *Daily Mail*, 17 Oct. 1891, 8. See also her third person vignette about a lonely wife with a little boy and infant daughter whose "drummer" (salesman) husband is on the road. Ibid., 4 Oct. 1890, 5.

17. In 1884 (as "Edward J."), 1885 and from 1888 to 1905, E.J. Watkins is listed as a commercial traveller and, later, foreman, for a dry goods company in the Toronto City Directory.

18. Gartshore-Waterous Interview.

19. PAC K.B.C. Photo Collection, A-93, No. 4. A similar photo identifies him as E.J. Watkins, John B. Gartshore's maternal grandfather. Ibid., No. 14.

20. See "He and She," and other untitled fragments in PAC K.B.C. Papers, Vol 2, Files 11, 26, 27, 29. See also "A Pair of Gray Gloves," written by Kathleen Blake Coleman for *Canadian Magazine*, in Vol. 2, File 20.

21. Five was the usual entrance age for kindergarten, which became part of the Ontario public school system in 1887. Neil Sutherland, *Children in English-Canadian Society* (University of Toronto Press 1976), 174.

22. Gartshore-Waterous Interview. The Toronto city directories for 1890 to 1893 give E.J. Watkins' addresses as being in the general area of Parkdale, near High Park or, alternately, closer to downtown. Kit mentioned taking a streetcar from Parkdale to the *Daily Mail* building on King Street, but it could have been before the break up. *Daily Mail*, 25 Jan. 1890, 5.

23. PAC K.B.C. Papers, Vol. 1, File 4, note dated 12 Oct. 1896. She also kept a letter "Teddie" wrote to "Santy" in the same file. Kit later told her readers that her children often called her "Br'er." Response to "Dorrie R.," *Mail and Empire*, 7 May, 1898, Part 2, 5.

24. Gartshore-Waterous Interview.

25. "My removal" may refer to her move to the convent. PAC K.B.C. Papers, Vol. 2, File 38. Confirmed Gartshore—Waterous Interview.

26. Information supplied by Sister Eleanor O'Meara, Archivist, Loretto Abbey, Toronto. In one of her later columns, Kit wrote about graduation exercises at Loretto Abbey, which involved "Patsy." *Mail and Empire*, 25 Dec. 1897, 4.

27. Kit said she had done that but did not name the newspaper or year. *Daily Mail*, 7 Oct. 1893, 5. Her correspondence section in the "Kingdom" started off as a graphology feature, but she had to give

up hand writing analysis because she was deluged with requests. Ibid., 16 Aug 1890, 5.

28. Response to "Elizabeth Kar or Kat," *Mail and Empire*, 26 June 1909, pp. 20-21.

29. Sheppard wrote as "Don," *Saturday Night*, 6 Sept. 1890, 1. Kit gave him full credit for helping her. *Mail and Empire*, 2 June 1900, 17. See also Ross Harkness, *J.E. Atkinson of the Star* (Toronto: University of Toronto Press 1963), 16.

30. Kit, "The Old Organ Grinder," *Saturday Night*, 10 Aug. 1889, 8. Kathleen kept the clipping and gave it to her son. "First lines I ever wrote published Aug. 10, 1889."—"For Thady—My very first bit of writing. In memoriam old days and poor Papa." PAC K.B.C. Papers, Vol. 1, File 14. Kit wrote that her proud father kept a copy of "The Old Organ Grinder" in his pocketbook. Response to "Bab," *Daily Mail*, 29 Apr. 1893, 8; *Mail and Empire*, 13 April 1895, 6.

31. Kit, "The French Revolution," *Saturday Night*, 17 Aug. 1889, 3; Kit, "A True Story," *Saturday Night*, 24 Aug. 1889, 4.

32. *Daily Mail*, 26 October 1889, 5.

33. Krout, op cit. Krout does not describe the article but it may have been based on the ancient version in which Adam's first wife, the assertive Lillith, is banished from the Garden of Eden and replaced by the more compliant Eve. Mary Daley, *Gyn/Ecology* (Boston: Beacon Press 1978), 86n.

34. Carman Cumming, "The Toronto *Daily Mail*, Edward Farrer, and the Question of Canadian-American Union," in *Journal of Canadian Studies*, Vol. 24, No. 1 (Spring 1989).

35. *Daily Mail*, 21 June 1890, 5.

36. Response to "Pussy," Ibid., 4 Oct. 1890, 5.

37. Ibid., 11 Oct. 1890, 5.

38. Response to "Miss McDuff," Ibid., 9 May 1891, 11. Her uncle, Father Burke, claimed to be descended from the same Irish king, but never pretended he was more than the son of a baker. The family was of mixed Protestant/Roman Catholic ancestry. Fitz-patrick, Vol. 1, pp. 1-3; 330.

39. See for example, *Mail and Empire*, 26 Mar. 1904, 20; manuscripts in PAC K.B.C. Papers, Vol. 2, Files 12-18; and "A Ban Delish: An Irish Sketch By Kit," *Mail and Empire Special Christmas Edition*, 1898 (incomplete copy). Ibid., Vol 4. File 3.

40. *Daily Mail*, 11 Apr. 1891, 5.

41. PAC K.B.C. Papers, Vol. 2, Files 13-18, outline and manuscripts marked "Chapter Eight" and "Chapter Nine."

42. Response to "J'Attends," *Mail and Empire*, 4 May 1907, 18. The "sunbeam" and "hoyden"—two extremes of Victorian girlhood por-

trayed in much of the literature of the time—are discussed in Deborah Gorham, *The Victorian Girl and the Feminine Ideal* (Indiana University Press 1982), Chapter 3.

43. *Daily Mail*, 2 Aug. 1890, 8.
44. Gorham, *The Victorian Girl*, pp. 21, 38, 41.
45. *Daily Mail*, 15 Aug. 1891, 5; 30 July, 1892, 8; Hamilton *Herald*, 28 Mar. 1914, 9.
46. *Daily Mail*, 23 May 1891, 5; *Mail and Empire*, 2 Jan. 1904, 16; PAC K.B.C. Papers, Vol. 2, Files 12-18.
47. Response to "The Professor," *Daily Mail*, 4 Feb. 1893, 8. She defended the use of a nom-de-plume, saying it protected a writer's privacy and provided a cover in case of literary failure. Response to "Verb Sap," Ibid., 14 Mar. 1891, 5.
48. *Mail and Empire*, 4 Dec. 1897, Part 2, 4; Fitz-patrick, Vol. 1, pp. 336, 354, fn1; Vol. 2, pp. 300-301, 316.
49. Response to "A Lover," *Mail and Empire*, 14 April 1900, Part 2, 5.
50. Fitz-patrick, Vol. 1, pp. vi-vii, 37, 57, 76, 96, 188-190; Vol. 2, 4.
51. Ibid., Vol. 2, pp. 50-59, 123, 175, 265, 272.
52. Ibid., Vol. 2, pp. 126, 230.
53. From a margin note written in her hand on a copy of her uncle's biography, now in the possession of her granddaughter, Kit Waterous. The author, W.J. Fitz-patrick, recorded the profound grief of the funeral crowd. He did not mention Kathleen or her behaviour directly but notes "...the grief shown by his sister was in high degree affecting." Fitz-patrick, Vol. 2, pp. 394-396. The word "sister" has been inked out in Kit Waterous' copy.
54. *Daily Mail*, 11 Jan. 1890, 5. Father Burke died of his chronic stomach ailment at age 51. Fitz-patrick, Vol. 2, pp. 172-173; 388-391. Kathleen later wrote a ghost story about a dead priest who bears a striking resemblance to Father Burke. PAC K.B.C. Papers, Vol. 2, File 22, "The Priest" and its plot outline.
55. Gorham, *The Victorian Girl*, 48.
56. *Daily Mail*, 21 June 1890, 5. See also a similar description of the mother in "Her Homecoming," PAC K.B.C. Papers, Vol. 2, File 12. The story was published in *Canada Monthly*, Apr. 1915, 391.
57. Response to "Howard," *Daily Mail*, 28 June 1890, 5. Father Burke's biographer mentions Mary Burke's musical ability but not her blindness. Fitz-patrick, Vol. 1, 17.
58. Gorham, *The Victorian Girl*, 47.
59. *Daily Mail*, 27 Dec. 1890, 5. The real-life Mary Burke was taught charity by her own deeply-religious mother. Fitz-patrick, Vol. 1, pp. 45-47.

60. Response to "No. 27," *Daily Mail*, 13 Aug. 1892, 8. See also, response to "Mrs. D.P.S. (Oil Springs)," Hamilton *Herald*, 20 July 1912, 7.
61. *Daily Mail*, 18 Oct. 1890, 5; Ibid., 5 Sept. 1891, 5; Ibid., 5 Dec. 1891, 9.
62. Ibid., 17 Oct. 1891, 5.
63. Ibid., 17 Oct. 1891, 5, and a somewhat different version, 18 June 1892, 8. The unrest was over ownership and control of Irish land. See Edward Normand, *A History of Ireland* (London: Allan Lane—The Penguin Press 1971), Chapter 8.
64. *Daily Mail*, 14 Feb. 1891, 5. "Rufus" also appears in Kathleen Blake Watkins, "The Secret Meeting And What Came Of It." PAC K.B.C. Papers, Vol 2, File 23.
65. *Daily Mail*, 22 Mar. 1890, 5.
66. Ibid., 12 April 1890, 5.
67. She always insisted that she never made up any of her letters. See for example Ibid., 15 Aug. 1891, 5.
68. There were numerous references, including Ibid., 3 May 1890, 5; Ibid., 14 June 1890, 5; Ibid., 23 Aug. 1890, 8.
69. Ibid,. 4 Oct. 1890, 5; Ibid., 8 Nov. 1890, 5 and Ibid., 13 Dec. 1890, 5.
70. Ibid., 27 Sept. 1890, pp. 5, 9.
71. Ibid., 2 Aug. 1890, 5.
72. Response to "Massage," Ibid., 12 July 1890, 5; response to "Admirer," Ibid., 21 July 1890, 5; Ibid., 1 Nov. 1890, 5.
73. Ibid., 3 May 1890, 5.
74. Ibid., 3 Sept. 1892, 5. "Theodocia" later died. Response to "An Old Woman," *Mail and Empire*, 25 Dec. 1897, Part 2, 6.
75. *Daily Mail*, 20 Sept. 1890, 5.
76. Ibid., 6 Dec. 1890, 5.
77. Ibid., 1 Nov. 1890, 5.
78. Ibid., 8 Nov. 1890, 5. She was not always consistent in this. See Ibid., 4 Jan. 1890, 5.
79. Ibid,. 28 Feb. 1891, 5.
80. Ibid., 14 Feb. 1891, 5.
81. Response to "Caesar," Ibid., 2 May 1891, 9.
82. Response to "Old Reader," Ibid., 2 Aug. 1890, 8.
83. Response to "Lorna Doone," Ibid., 1 Nov. 1890, 5.
84. Normand, Chapters 8 and 9.
85. *Daily Mail*, 20 Dec. 1890, 5. Kit later claimed that Parnell had often been a guest at her father's table. Ibid., 6 Aug. 1892, 8.
86. Ibid,. 26 Nov. 1892, 8.
87. Ibid., 28 Feb. 1891, 5.
88. Cumming, op. cit.
89. Ramsay Cook, *The Regenerators, Social Criticism in Late Victorian Canada* (Toronto: University of Toronto Press 1985), pp. 139-142.

90. *Daily Mail* 17 Oct. 1891, 5.
91. Ibid., 31 Oct. 1891, 8.
92. Cumming, 134.
93. *Daily Mail*, 17 Jan. 1891, 5.
94. See, for example, response to "Molly," Ibid., 22 Nov. 1890, 5.
95. Ibid., 11 Jan. 1890, 5.
96. Response to "Pere Hyacinth," Ibid., 5 July 1890, 8.
97. *Mail and Empire*, 4 Dec. 1897, Part 2, 5.
98. Response to "Little Boy Blue," *Daily Mail*, 12 July 1890, 5.
99. Response to "Fraulein," Ibid., 18 Oct. 1890, 5. Her uncle's biographer wrote that Father Burke was anti-Darwin, but Kathleen's notes in her granddaughter's copy of the book read: "Church, Church, Church, (unintelligible) fiend of a Church... These were not uncle's thoughts." Fitz-patrick, Vol. 2, pp. 167-168. Father Burke believed that science and religion were compatible. Rochford (ed.), *Father Burke's Sermons and Lectures*, pp. 234-267.
100. *Daily Mail*, 18 Oct. 1890, 5.
101. Question mark hers. Ibid., 25 Oct. 1890, 5.
102. Ed Caudill, "A Content Analysis of Press Views of Darwin's Evolution Theory, 1860-1925" in *Journalism Quarterly*, Winter 1987, pp. 782-786.
103. Cook, *The Regenerators*, pp. 9-15.
104. Susan E. Houston, "Victorian Origins of Juvenile Delinquency," in *History of Education Quarterly*, Vol. XII, June 1972, pp. 254-280. See also Houston, "Waifs and Strays of a Late Victorian City: Juvenile Delinquents in Toronto," in Joy Parr (ed.), *The Family in Canadian History* (Toronto: McClelland and Stewart 1982). Contemporary sources include J.J. Kelso, *Early History of the Humane and Children's Aid Movement in Ontario* (Toronto: King's Printer L.K. Cameron 1911) and C.S. Clark, *Of Toronto the Good: The Queen City of Canada As It Is* (Toronto: Toronto Publishing Company 1898 repr. Coles Publishing 1970).
105. Response to "Mater," *Daily Mail*, 7 Nov. 1891, 5.
106. Houston, "Waifs and Strays" op. cit.; W.R. Morrison, "Their Proper Sphere: Feminism, the Family and Child-Centred Social Reform in Ontario, 1885-1900," in *Ontario History*, Vol. LXVIII, Nos. 1 and 2, Mar. and June 1976; Sutherland, *Children In English-Canadian Society*.
107. *Daily Mail*, 7 Mar. 1891, 5.
108. Ibid., 18 Apr. 1891, 5.
109. See for example Ibid., 27 Sept. 1890, 5.
110. Ibid., 22 Nov. 1890, 5.
111. Ibid., 14 Mar. 1891, 5.
112. Response to "Hazeldean," Ibid., 5 Sept. 1891, 5.

113. Ibid., 12 Sept. 1891, 5.
114. Ibid., 4 July 1891, 5.
115. Response to "J.J.B.," *Mail and Empire,* 9 Feb. 1895, 5; Ibid., 18 Jan. 1896, 5.
116. Objectivity is "the separation of facts from values." Schudson, 5.
117. *Daily Mail,* 27 Apr. 1893, 8.
118. Response to "Brixton," Ibid., 7 Feb. 1891, 5. Kathleen kept an article, however, in which his writing was unfavorably compared with hers. PAC K.B.C. Papers, Vol. 3, File 1, unidentified clipping.
119. *Daily Mail,* 12 Sept. 1891, 6; *Mail and Empire* Saturday Supplement, 12 Oct. 1895, 5; Kit's response to "P.P.C.," Ibid., 14 Dec. 1895, 6.
120. Response to "H.F.," *Daily Mail,* 8 Nov. 1890, 5; response to "Santa Catalina," Ibid., 24 Dec. 1892, 8.
121. Ibid., 25 Apr. 1891, 9.
122. Response to "Cosmopolitan," Ibid., 11 Feb. 1893, 8.
123. Ibid., 24 June 1893, 5.
124. *Grip,* Vol. XXXVI, No. 3 (17 Jan. 1891), pp. 34-38. The following week, it analyzed "Kitt's" signature, a reference to her interest in graphology. Ibid., No. 4 (24 Jan. 1891), 52.
125. *Daily Mail,* 31 Jan. 1891, 5. Bengough is discussed by Cook, *The Regenerators,* Ch. 8.
126. One hot week in August 1891, she received 104 letters. Responses to "Bernard Hope" and "Irish Willow," *Daily Mail,* 15 Aug. 1891, 11.
127. Ibid., 14 Feb. 1891, 5.
128. Response to "Balmaceda," Ibid., 14 Nov. 1891, 5.
129. Response to "Dame Durden," Ibid., 15 Nov. 1890, 5.
130. Ibid., 28 Feb. 1891, 5.

CHAPTER 2
MIXED MESSAGES

Kit's earliest work revealed an underlying anxiety over what she should write about for Canadian women and how to please them. When she introduced "Our Letter Club" in the spring of 1890, she made it clear that she was not content merely to borrow her ideas from articles in American publications and wanted to know what interested her own audience. She suggested marriage, women's rights and wrongs, temperance and anything else most readers would find interesting.[1] But it became evident that these discussions had to be conducted only in certain acceptable ways in the "Kingdom," especially when they threatened the status quo between the sexes.

Kit rebelled against some strictures and accepted others. Although she had a strong individualistic streak, she was inconsistent in her views on women's rights and also tended to trivialize them. Her stance was influenced by the limited interest in the subject among her readers and the dismissive attitude toward it among her male, professional peers, particularly at the *Daily Mail*.

The women's movement had been a fact of nineteenth century life for several decades, bringing with it a word that was commonplace by the 1890s—"feminist"—meaning a woman who wanted autonomy for herself as an individual as well as for the female sex as a whole.[2] By 1889, the Women's Franchise League in Britain was advocating the

vote for all women, not just those who were single or widowed, which was the position advocated as more judicious
by conservative suffrage groups.[3] In Canada, as in the
United States, the movement consisted mainly of professional and self-supporting women, or wives of men with
good incomes. It embraced separate groups, some of them
feminists who wanted total educational and occupational
equality with men, but most being well-educated, Anglo-
Saxon, Protestant women and men who had overlapping
memberships in several different social reform
organizations.[4]

Among the main advocates of women's suffrage, for
example, were various branches of the Women's Christian
Temperance Union, which wanted women to have the vote
in order to bring about an end to licensed saloons and the
selling of liquor. The WCTU women blamed alcohol for
many social evils, including wife-battering. The vote would
give them extended power to protect their homes through
social control.[5]

cliché

Legislators saw no urgency about granting women the
vote, and with good reason. As suffrage chronicler
Catherine Cleverdon has pointed out, the task of the
women suffrage activists "was made doubly onerous by the
apathy, if not outright hostility"[6] they often met in other
women. Many people still held the Victorian notion that
women were too weak to participate in political excitement
and would only compromise their femininity and maternalism if they tried.

Public resistance did not deter the women's rights activists, however. During the 1880s in Ontario, there had been
some agitation, mostly from small temperance groups, for
laws extending the municipal and provincial franchises to
unmarried women at least. In addition, the Toronto
Women's Suffrage Association, under the leadership of
Doctor Emily Stowe, devoted itself to the advancement of
women in education and the professions, particularly medicine, as well as to suffrage. In 1889, after a lull in its activity,
its leaders established the Dominion Women's

A typical title illustration from Kit's page in the *Mail*, Spring 1894.

Kit tries to answer her readers' letters amid spring cleaning chaos.
From the *Daily Mail*, 1892.

Enfranchisement Association and, within a year, branches began to spring up in various Ontario towns. The DWEA continued to fight for the provincial franchise into the early 1890s, but to no avail.[7] It took another twenty-five years or more for Canadian women to win the federal and provincial votes in Canada.

Kit was very slow to embrace the cause. Although there had been alcoholism in her family,[8] she was not a temperance advocate and, in fact, resented any attempts by reformers to impose their views on her or anyone else.[9] As a well-educated woman who worked outside the home, she was aware that men did not treat women fairly but, unlike many of her female colleagues,[10] was reluctant to take on the role of newspaper crusader for most causes[11] and quickly learned not to promote such a marginal one as suffrage. She did, however, support equal pay for most women, although her attitude toward those of the working class tended to be patronizing.

In the meantime, there was a debate in the North American newspaper industry over suitable content for the women's pages. Editors—and some women journalists— were balking at discussions about contentious issues such as equal pay, suffrage and sexual autonomy, preferring to attract advertising with articles about fashion, beauty and interior decorating. One week, an enthusiastic Kit reported a "conversation" she had with a "bright little" American journalist, who declared it was not the place of women's page writers to "...mount the pedestal and condescend to the rest of the world and preach moral little maxims and write elevating articles."[12] Kit's friend was referring to a debate in the *New York Herald* on women's pages, which began with a discussion among members of the Sorosis Society,[13] a group of feminist professional women. The membership included a number of journalists, who revealed that male editors often censored their attempts to add intellectual content to their women's page.[14] One of the strongest letters in response to the article came from "Helen Watterson," a freelance writer, who insisted that women readers wanted to know about changes in all areas affecting women around the world, whether it be in the arts, science, the law or business.

> But they want more than this even. They want to be treated with respect...women are tired of being patronized and besmirched by turns. They are tired of being jeered at and ridiculed for every intellectual, social, or moral project they undertake.. Women want clean, wise, dignified, respectful, helpful newspaper stuff. The wisest editor is he who will provide it. [15]

Kit's own feeling—based on letters from her readers— was that most of them wanted a mix of the serious and the light in the "Kingdom," [16] and she complied with a formula that did not change over the years. She was not alone in this. Other journalists, including two temperance supporters who believed women should have the vote, also wrote with their audiences in mind. Elmira Elliott ("Madge Merton"), of the Toronto *Globe* discussed lightly provocative topics such as "What is beauty?" in women and men, and friendship between women. [17] Alice Fenton Freeman ("Faith Fenton") of the Conservative party newspaper, the Toronto *Empire*, had a Saturday page very similar to Kit's, in which she wrote short paragraphs on items of general interest and published poetry and syndicated fashion notes. [18]

Kit followed the dictates of her editor in her choice of suitable women's page material, even when supposedly soliciting her readers' opinions:

> Do you want accounts of gay doings or do you like dear little moral platitudes in stained glass attitudes best—or a mixture of both? I would oftener write platitudes if I thought you cared about them, but our editor says you don't. "Not too much preaching," is the axiom. "Women and girls like to be amused." It is for you to say, my dears. I'm the cook (God help me!) [19]

But her belief that women, whether they eventually married or not, had a right to earn a living led her to support one controversial plank of the feminist platform, at least, and that was equal pay. It was a demand that was slowly earning some support in Canadian society. The DWEA, for example, promoted "Equal Pay for Equal Labour" as did some Protestant churches on the grounds that it would improve the health of working mothers.[20] The more outspoken feminists wrote letters about it to newspaper editors. "Breadwinner," for example, believed that low wages forced women into marriage, which she equated with legalized prostitution, while "W" declared that women had the right to work in the occupations of their choice.[21]

Several prominent women journalists also supported equal pay, some with reservations. Agnes Maule Machar was an early believer while the younger Elmira Elliott ("Madge Merton") of the Toronto *Globe* felt it was a matter of "common justice." Sara Jeannette Duncan, who was generally supportive of working women, equivocated, saying that equality with men in the work place depended on what the labour market could bear.[22]

Kit declared her support after receiving a tirade from "Truth-seeker," who did not think women should work outside the home at all. His letter was too much for the journalist, who bluntly interjected in parentheses, arguing his every point:

> There are plenty of men to do all the work—(N.B.— Maybe. But some of them are lazy and incompetent, or the woman wouldn't have got to do it) ...men have to take less for doing those things— (N.B.— And women have to take less than the merest midget of a man, though she may do better work) ...all men would have work and plenty of it— (N.B.—While the lunatic asylum would be filled with women made crazy through the monotonous slavery of housework without any intellectual holidays).... If I am right, I want someone to take up the battle with me and let us fight for the day women will no longer be slaves—(N.B.—Just listen to the man, after binding us to washing dishes or making home-made gowns all our lives!)— and every woman will be the possessor of a bright, happy home— (N.B.— With a lord and master like you I suppose. No, no.)[23]

She later explained that she was a woman:

> ...who sincerely advocates the raising of wages for female labour, and honestly thinks that if a woman works, even in those ways too long closed to her by men, woman should be paid accordingly, and honoured, too, if she can help in ever so small a way the partner she has chosen for life, or keep herself independently, earning sufficient to place her above the temptations offered her by men.[24]

Within limits, Kit encouraged any woman who wanted to work to make her living, whether she wanted a profession or a job in domestic service. Quite a number of her readers were interested in being journalists like herself and she was always ready with encouragement and advice, even though there were not a lot of opportunities outside of the women's pages.[25] Kit told one aspiring journalist that, although some newspapermen would be supportive of her, generally "Men deplore this 'rushing into print' of women. They are condescending, patronizing or mercilessly sarcastic..."[26]

Her own advice was practical and realistic. She believed that a woman could be a success in journalism, as long as she pleased her editors and kept the demands of the journalistic market in mind. She warned her feminist readers not to present editors with suffragist tracts, but woo them with light features, because that was what was expected of female newcomers.[27] And while she encouraged women to aspire to news reporting, a rough-and-ready male occupation at the time,[28] she also reminded them that excellent spelling and grammar was the mark of "a lady."[29]

Kit could sometimes be flippant about women's aspirations to enter professions dominated by men—she once declared that females would make good lawyers because they had a talent for talking[30]—but she gradually became more supportive when she realized how many women were interested in these fields, particularly medicine.[31] By 1890, several Canadian universities and medical schools were offering medical training to women who, nevertheless, still faced a great deal of opposition within the profession.[32] Kit well understood that many male physicians' antagonism toward women doctors was based on economic factors, even if she felt compelled to be cautious in saying so:

> JANE thinks women doctors should not attend on men. I agree with her, but Jane wishes women to attend the same lectures, pocket the same fees, stand the same examinations as men. You are welcome to your views of the questions, Jane, but I'll keep mine close "in mine breast" and so avert the hysterical storm of—something that would break over my head if I make them public. Money is at the bottom of it, and why shouldn't women make all they can?[33]

Women who were not ambitious to enter the male-dominated professions had the well-established options of school teaching and nursing. By 1900, most of the elementary school teachers in Canada were women, who earned little recognition or pay; women going into nursing were similarly exploited.[34] Kit had her reservations about both fields. They were good training grounds for motherhood, she wrote, but teaching paid poorly[35] and nursing was not for the sentimental or fainthearted, but involved rigorous training and hard work.[36] She found that the hardest women to advise were the many older, middle-class unfortunates who had found themselves, through the death, illness or desertion of their husbands, in dire financial straits. She sympathized greatly and tried to make helpful suggestions, advising one woman, for example, to open a boarding-house.[37] Boardinghouses were commonly used as accommodation by nineteenth century working men and women and keeping one was an option which would allow the woman to keep her social status, work at home and still earn a living.[38]

In her writing about working-class women and work, Kit, as both a gentlewoman and a working mother, was often torn by her efforts to present both sides of the boss/employee question, efforts which resulted in some inconsistency and confusion in her essays. In one, for example, she appeared to be appalled at the long hours and low pay of women working in factories and shops and painted a

Dickensian portrait of one "working girl" designed to elicit her readers' attention and sympathy:

> A slight lame girl in a shabby black gown was toiling wearily up the long staircase after her day's work was done. Her face was pallid with that grey look upon it that comes from confinement, want of proper rest and lack of bathing. As she limped past on her way to her room in the roof, one could see what a frail, delicate little creature she was.

The young woman worked from eight in the morning to five in the evening, finishing button holes on new footwear for seven cents per hundred. She earned whatever her speed and agility dictated—barely enough money to cover her board of two dollars a week.[39]

Although Kit was sympathetic, she did not question the economic system that exploited the young woman. Instead, she claimed that it was women who worked simply for something to do before they got married, and who were often incompetent, who lowered the standard of wages for the rest. To merit equal pay and fair treatment, women had to adopt the male model of business behaviour. For example, she exhorted female office workers not to sulk, as an unnamed male boss complained they invariably did, when they were being corrected. She did not entirely spare employers from criticism, however. She declared that some men, known in their communities for their generous donations to charity, were actually hypocrites because they underpaid their female employees, especially those they knew would work just as hard as a man for a lower wage.[40]

In another essay, a few weeks later, Kit became a little bolder in her defence of working women. She risked alienating some of the *Mail's* advertisers by urging a consumer boycott of Saturday afternoon and evening shopping. She had received from "Viola," a shop girl, a letter "full of unconscious pathos...the cry of one more courageous than others of her class." "Viola" complained that shop girls had to work until eleven p.m. on Saturdays, do without proper meals and bear the cruel barbs of impatient shop-keepers. Kit felt that young women should not be kept standing behind counters for hours at a time—probably because she feared for their reproductive organs[41]—and urged her readers to support early closing on Saturdays.[42] "Viola" wrote again, thanking Kit and expressing the powerlessness of her own position: "...we girls are afraid to start the ball rolling in the early closing matter, lest we get a note in our pay envelopes and find ourselves without a situation, with only $2.50 in our purse." Kit, in response, castigated the shop-keepers for paying "starvation wages" and urged them to "try to get a little more humanity into your systems." She asked for their comments in return, but none were forthcoming.[43]

The only group that did not need equal wages, she felt, were domestic servants, the largest single group of female employees in Canada. In 1891, they accounted for 41 per cent of the national female labour force, with Ontario close to the national average. Wages were about five to six dollars a month in rural areas and up to twenty dollars in the cities and towns.[44] Kit argued that because domestic servants were provided with room and board by their employers, they were in a more comfortable and certainly safer environment than those women who had to work alongside men in shops and factories.[45] At the time, there was a great deal of community concern about the working woman's purity in a mixed sex environment,[46] but it did not seem to occur to Kit that domestics might be in just as much danger from sexual advances made by male members of a household as they might be from a factory boss or foreman.

Despite the inventions of the industrial revolution outside the home, inside it, housekeeping was still an "arduous," full-time job[47] which, along with child-rearing, was seen as the responsibility of women. The "domestic problem"— getting good help—was a constantly discussed theme in the women's pages of newspapers and magazines, club women's deliberations and private letters.[48]

Many middle-class women wrote to Kit about their domestic problems, and the journalist did her part by encouraging young, working-class women who needed employment to become maids.[49] She wrote that she had some experience "working out" herself, when she first came to Canada, and "would not be without the experience for anything you could offer me."[50] But she was very patronizing in her attitude toward domestics, as were other women writers.[51] Kit sometimes insulted these workers, many of whom were immigrants from the British Isles,[52] by depicting them as ignorant peasant stereotypes, particularly the Irish "Bridget."[53] From time to time, however, she would attempt to present both sides of the ongoing struggle between mistress and maid.

It was difficult to persuade working-class women to choose domestic service over life in the factories, where the hours and pay were better. In private homes, maids were constantly "on call," were often fed inadequately and provided with poor sleeping accommodations in damp basements or cramped attics. They were usually lonely as well because they were socially isolated from the families for whom they worked, especially in the cities.[54]

Kit scolded mistresses who treated their servants badly and advocated "give and take" and "elasticity in household arrangements." But she did not believe in social mixing and, ever status-conscious, insisted that maids wear uniforms whether they wanted to or not.[55] Servants, as well as mistresses, praised her for her more equitable essays on the question. Wrote "A Nurse Girl": "You are the only one I ever knew who talked sense in the papers."[56]

Although Kit saw herself as championing the case of working women everywhere and supported equal pay and fair working conditions, her public position on other aspects of women's rights—notably suffrage and sexual autonomy—was antagonistic. It is difficult to understand her inconsistency, but it appears that she was influenced by her editors and readers in what she wrote and perhaps by her own upbringing as well.

She may have been a private supporter of the vote for women, but it appears that she tested the public waters and found them distinctly cool before she decided that suffrage

was not a popular topic among her readers. She first mentioned it—favourably—about three months after she began
working at the *Daily Mail*. An arrogant Toronto alderman
had declared that women had no business doing their shopping at night because they took up too many streetcar seats,
which should be reserved for weary working men. Kit
retorted that most mothers were too busy with their children
to do their shopping during the day and added indignantly,
"Oh, I wish women could vote!"[57]

The following week, she reviewed a new Canadian book,
Woman, Her Character, Culture and Calling. She noted suffrage
leader Augusta Stowe Gullen's "encouraging and liberal"
chapter on "Women in the Study and Practice of Medicine"
and commented that "the articles on Higher Education of
Woman and the Suffrage are treated with earnestness and
liberality." She agreed with the authors that "fighting for
women is really fighting for men."[58]

Several months later, on 12 June and 13 June 1890, the
Dominion Women's Enfranchisement Association held a
convention in Toronto during which the audience of over
100 heard speakers such as Doctor Emily Stowe, the
Reverend Anna Shaw, M.D. of the United States and several male "experts" discuss women's educational, occupational and political aspirations.[59] Kit did not cover the conference in "Woman's Kingdom"—possibly because the
Mail had already done so on its news pages[60]—but urged
her readers to send her letters on women's rights.[61] She
received only three, the first from "Pollie," who she quoted
at length:

> Giving women the ballot would not fail to have a beneficial
> effect on the future of Canada. If woman's indirect influence
> has in most cases been on the side of good, how much more
> her direct influence will be felt when she has a voice in mak-
> ing the laws of her country. She will then see to it that we
> have laws to amend the purity and happiness of her home...
> Canadian future statesmen,—by having less temptation to
> contend with, would become more intelligent, for believe me,
> Kit, one half the men—politically speaking—are densely
> ignorant.

Kit withheld her own comments, but exhorted her apparently reluctant readers to get in on the debate:

> Are you afraid of the subject? For pity's sake be afraid of nothing or nobody when you have views to state. Don't mind what men say. They talk sometimes as if it were a sin to write, unless the writing be of a very superior order...Pouf! Nonsense.[62]

But she received only two other letters, both of them anti-suffrage. First she quoted the one she received from "G.B.G.," a man:

> ...who thanks the gods that "Canadian women have as yet escaped from the pernicious effect of this female mania of the age, which to a great degree springs from discontent and disappointment...We see (American) women jostle their way into public offices and other vocations of men with the conspicuous and lamentable result that they lose after a time the gentleness that made them lovable while they confined their attentions to former occupations and household duties."

In the second letter, "Katherine" wrote that women did not know enough about the law to vote, and did not care enough about the issue to learn. Kit quoted her, too:

> ...do you really think that anything very material will be gained by women voting as their husbands, fathers and brothers wish them to, for by voting with their hearts, not their heads, will dictate to the creation of many a family jar. I do not.

Both writers were afraid that the line between the genders was becoming too confused, that women were turning masculine and men effeminate. It was a common anti-feminist anxiety that was often expressed in newspaper or magazine articles about the "masculine girl," who was usually shown dressed in men's clothing, at least above the waist.[63]

Kit agreed with the letters, particularly "G.B.G.'s" "able and logical" one. She went on to denounce the "masculine" woman, and particularly the "platform woman...(who)...almost always becomes an intolerable nuisance, loses a great deal of refinement and can hardly help becoming coarse." In that week's muddled and inconsistent "Kingdom," she

61

strongly supported women's intellectual equality with men, but not their political aspirations, which would detract from their maternal natures.

> Do not, dear girls, in the glare of Women's Rights; or the suffrage, the emancipation of the sex, or any other of these advanced (?) movements, lose sight of the exquisite home virtues, the self-sacrifice, gentleness and wonderful moral courage which is as far above the physical attribute as the stars are above the earth.[64]

At the same time, however, she told "Elaine" that a woman should try to cultivate her mind as much as a man would. She did not explain how women could be intellectual but not intelligent enough to decide for themselves the best candidate in an election. But it is clear that she equated politics with masculinity and unladylike behaviour.[65] Kit preferred to believe that it wasn't necessary for women to become politically active, that they were already emancipating themselves, discreetly, by their accomplishments. As she explained later to one of her correspondents, "... woman is surely but quietly doing all this for herself—and minding the home too."[66]

Kit was not the only woman journalist who balked at activism. A contributor to the *Globe's* women's page, "Marguerite," declared: "This strife between men and women is absurd and childish, but it is worse than that, it is absolutely wicked."[67] On the other hand, several women journalists declared themselves in favour of suffrage. They included Sara Jeannette Duncan, who was not herself involved in the women's movement,[68] freelance writer Agnes Maule Machar[69] and Alice Fenton Freeman of the Toronto *Empire*. Freeman felt it was her professional duty to publicize movement activities, for example, the 1893 International Women's Congress in Chicago, which she attended as both a delegate for the Women's Christian Temperance Union[70] and as a journalist:

> I think it is due our Canadian women—the many women of home-work and home ties who need the inspiration that such a gathering gives—that they should have as full an

account as possible of this conference. The time for ridiculing such gatherings has long gone by.[71]

Unlike Freeman, Kit remained aloof from the women's movement. She may have been responding not just to her own personal biases but to those of her readers and the editors of the *Daily Mail*. She claimed that she received far more letters from readers on "why men don't marry" and "flirting" than she did on the vote or other stimulating issues, a situation which often disappointed the journalist, who usually liked a good, intellectual discussion.[72]

She was also aware that suffrage was not high on the priority list of most editors, especially her own. During the DWEA conference in Toronto, most of the local dailies expressed respect for the delegates, but stopped short of supporting suffrage.[73] The *Daily Mail* was more outspoken in its opposition than most, declaring that it was "idle" of the delegates to expect the vote soon in Canada. "There is in the Dominion a strong aversion to the dragging of women into politics." No matter how intellectual the woman, the *Mail* believed, her proper place was in her home with her children.[74]

Kit may also have been influenced in her own attitude by her colleague and friend, H.H. Wiltshire ("The Flaneur"), a conservative man who was a vicious critic of feminists. During May 1891, he had an ongoing debate in his page about the emancipated woman, for whom he had little respect. "What is called in the cant of the time the movement for the independence of woman has produced a feminine breed that is primarily self-assertive and impertinent,"[75] he declared.

The next month, Wiltshire ran an anonymously written poem about two women, entitled "Woman and Her Rights," with illustrations. The activist woman was represented in both verse and drawing as tight-lipped, plain, and dissatisfied with her lot in life. The other, who did not seek her rights, was conventionally pretty, had a husband and children and "dreamt not of some path to mannish

heights.''[76] Kit never took "The Flaneur" to task for his anti-
woman sentiments, and later wrote that, with the exception
of the Irish Question, the two agreed on everything, including the traditional view of marriage and motherhood.[77]

Kit's susceptibility to male influence was inevitable, given
the power of men in newsrooms and the relative absence
of women, but there was another reason for her reliance on
the opinions of male colleagues. She did not then believe
that women—and particularly women journalists—could
be good friends and supporters to one another. She wrote
that true friendship between women was precious but
rare—like her own tender relationship with "Theodocia."[78]
But, among the "shrews" of the world, she counted "literary women" because, in her view, they were too critical of
each other and engaged in too much back-stabbing. She did
not explain why she wrote the following passage, but it
appears that someone, perhaps Kit herself, had been
accused of plagiarizing another woman's copy.

> "Literary" women are such sweet friends to each other, too.
> (Save the mark!) Nowadays, if a woman writes half a column
> for a newspaper she is dubbed "literary," and she watches
> every other "literary" woman closely and tries to make out
> that the other's work is mere plagiarism, and if she happens
> on a bit of gossip that she thinks she read in some other jour-
> nal, what a bonne bouche it is to her! How she goes about
> telling everyone she knows that "Bab" and "Mab" and "Mary
> March" (whose column you rather liked last week) stole that
> or this smart saying from the "Daily Wriggler" and never
> gave credit for it, and she writes (on a typewriter) to unfor-
> tunate "Mary March" and upbraids her with her sins, and
> next day she meets "Mary" at a literary tea, and fawns and
> my dears, and even kisses her, and takes vicious little notes
> about her dress and accent, and appearance to be circulated
> presently among their twenty or thirty friends. Bless the
> woman! Did she never sneak in a bit of unpretentious copy
> herself? Did she never drag someone else's idea forward, and
> deck and garnish and trim it to eke out her own weekly or
> daily column? Far better avoid "literary teas" and "literary"
> women if their friendship is like this.[79]

At the time, Kit's whole tone toward women in general lacked a sense of solidarity. She often portrayed men as superior to women, declaring that men were above gossiping[80] or that their love was nobler than women's.[81] That men were naturally superior to women was a commonly held, Victorian attitude,[82] but Kit risked offending her female readers when she actually admitted that she preferred the letters of men to those of women.[83] One of her correspondents, "Beth," felt that letters from men should not be published in the "Kingdom" at all:

> Look here, we girls don't want you to allow those conceited men to monopolize our Woman's sheet of THE MAIL, the dear (sic) knows they have every other corner they want to rage in; they are conceited enough to imagine, I suppose, that the girls cannot write letters, and they would jump at the chance to lord it over us, as they generally try to do...If I were you, Kit, I would keep those boys down a little, it is about time they were made to know their place.[84]

But Kit was proud that many males read her page and felt that, while it was mainly for women, men had their place in it "principally because so many women like to discuss matters with the sterner sex."[85]

One of the issues that attracted men as well as women to her page was "social purity," which a reader suggested as a topic for "Our Letter Club."[86] Social purity was a very complex issue and attracted proponents of all ideological stripes. The feminists among them believed that males had developed, in the words of historian Linda Gordon, "excessive sexual drives which contributed to the subjection of women and hence limited the development of the whole civilization." But the excessiveness of the drive, which was seen as social and not biological, could be eliminated and replaced with nobler activities. Chastity before marriage and monogamy, with some sexual abstinence during it for men as well as women, would bring an end to prostitution, pornography and venereal disease and eliminate any need for birth control and abortion. Most importantly, the accompanying concept of "voluntary motherhood"—the right to refuse sex—gave married women some control over what happened in the bedroom while allowing them to retain, at will, their status as mothers.[87]

At first, Kit got little response to the topic, except for queries as to exactly what social purity meant. But there was one provocative letter, from "Betsy Trotwood," who declared that, although she liked individual males:

> ...the majority of men are vile, utterly vile, and quite unworthy to associate with, much less marry, the majority of girls with whom they claim equality in the social scale ...there are some girls, I believe, Kit, who prefer wisdom, independence, happy freedom and contempt, to the ignorant bliss(?), the unconscious degradation and slavery of so many poor, sweet, confiding wives...I say that the most pitiful sight in the whole world is a loving bride.[88]

Kit was not convinced. As far as she was concerned, sexual morality was primarily the responsibility of the female, a common idea at the time,[89] and she claimed that she had known as many "noble, pure" men as women:

> That there are wretched wives, cowardly husbands, men who are true to no woman, who are false, brutal incarnate devils I know well. But I know, too, that no matter how low a man falls, there is a depth of degradation which he cannot reach; only a woman, a depraved fallen woman, can drop therein.[90]

The debate on social purity and related topics opened the journalist's eyes, however, to many men's sexual attitudes. Some of their letters to her, which she did not publish, revealed "unjust, savage, uncivilized views ...on women and womankind...My whole soul revolted against them." She also mentioned several "clever letters from ladies," who pointed out the double standards and inconsistencies in many men's logic and behaviour on the social purity issue.[91] Afterwards, her tendency to idealize men above women became tempered with a more realistic point of view. She decided that men were just as guilty of gossiping as women, boasted about their sexual conquests, and got over their romantic liaisons quickly,[92] while women could courageously bear for years their hidden anguish over broken love affairs. "How many hearts wear corsets!"[93]

Readers of both sexes confided their romantic secrets to Kit, who provided the socially approved advice they clearly expected, advice that would keep women and girls in particular, out of trouble. Usually, it did not deviate far from the strictures set down in the late Victorian guidance books and magazine columns, which promulgated the conventional wisdom that healthy, morally well-behaved young women made the best wives and mothers.

For example, some medical experts considered teenage girls to be particularly fragile because of menstruation, not just during their periods but for their entire adolescence.[94] Kit accepted this view and wrote that, while a girl should pursue an education, too much study and competition for marks at school could unbalance her mental equilibrium.[95] She was a proponent of fresh air and healthy exercise and, equating healthy good looks with attractiveness to the opposite sex, encouraged girls and young women to take up sports, such as archery and tennis.[96] They should also, she wrote, learn domestic skills in preparation for their future roles as wives and mothers.[97]

Her advice on courting and marriage stressed common sense as much as moral behaviour. She was not a prude, she declared, but, since appearances were all-important, single women should have chaperons and not be too careless with their kisses.[98] They should not rush into marriage with available but unsuitable men, especially if their suitors had habits or health problems that would hurt their future wives and children. Accordingly, she counselled "Jenny Wren" not to be swayed by a man who begged her to marry him and save him from his drinking problem[99] and scolded "Rosalie" for even thinking about marrying a man with an unspecified illness because he could pass it on to their children.[100]

But Kit did not always stick to the straight and narrow path of convention in her advice and comments. She declared that she herself had escaped the influence of that paragon of fashion, etiquette and public opinion, "Mrs. Grundy,"[101] and occasionally, the strength of some of her real feelings on controversial subjects showed. One was allowances for married women working at home. Kit believed that marriage was essentially a partnership of different but equal people and wives should be encouraged, within the domestic context, to be self-sufficient. Husbands should pay their wives set allowances, she declared, and let them spend it on the household without interference, for "...it is living in a state of slavery to be obliged to ask for fifty cents or a dollar, and then be questioned as to what she does with every cent of it."[102]

When some readers questioned her, she revealed her own independent streak, explaining that she herself would "rather go out charring or take in washing ...than be obliged to ask any man for money."[103] Both men and women took notice of what she wrote, and not all of them liked it. "Mary" told her that her married male friends "talked of 'Kit' and what their wives thought of that person....Some saw no good in such a discussion" about allowances.[104]

She even dared to question the sanctity of marriage itself, although she quickly had to bow to pressure and retract her comments. They concerned a case of wife-battering involving a Margaret Thompson of Hamilton, whose husband of forty years had kicked her black and blue. Kit reacted with outrage:

> A woman gives all she has to a man, her beauty, youth and virginity—her very soul almost, and he requites it with a kick when she is old and useless. Upon my word, sometimes the great enigma of why women should so suffer comes over me, until I can see no mercy for her, no justice, no decent charity upon this earth...No wonder women have more faith in immortality than men do. But for it no woman would elect to live her life out. I may be wrong. Some women are no doubt very happy. But the unhappiness so overheaps the happiness that I feel justified in speaking as I do.[105]

A month later, concerned that she had been "unwomanly," she did a complete about-face:

There is far too much venomous, bitter writing against men and marriage and all that. For heaven's sake, let us women try to retain our womanliness and hold fast to our belief in the honour and goodness of men and in love and all the sweet old beliefs that make the world as bright as they do—for is there not enough sorrow and bitterness?...If ever I wrote one bitter line, or suggested in any unwomanly manner that marriage and love were dismal failures, I sincerely regret it. I 'take it all back' for I am learning through the letters I get every day how very careful anyone who is writing for young girls and women ought to be, and how much we all need words of sympathy and encouragement. [106]

Although Kit later claimed that her editor allowed her to write, edit and revise her column "as I think fit,"[107] it is likely that either he or her readers had pressured her to retract. She extended her censorship to her readers and refused to publish "A Woman's" letter on marriage because it was "much too strong, and controversy does no good, but evil.." Undaunted, "A Woman" wrote back: "If you are a man you are a very mean one, and if you are a woman you are a very subservient woman."[108]

Judging from her replies in her correspondence column, however, many of Kit's readers supported the decision to censor any anti-male, anti-marriage comments.[109] They preferred to write to "Our Letter Club" about that paragon of virtue, the Ideal Woman. "Ruth" made it clear, in a letter Kit particularly liked, that moral responsibility was a prerequisite of success for the ideal woman writer: "We hail a woman as a literary star with pleasure when she presents truths that shall make us happier and nobler, and teach us how to ameliorate the evil and enhance the general good."[110]

As she matured as a journalist, however, Kit dealt more realistically with women's problems, including hidden ones, such as alcohol and drug abuse[111] and severe depression brought on by the boredom, drudgery and isolation of housework.[112] She understood that wives were financially dependent on their husbands so that, while she deplored the double standard of marital fidelity,[113] she warned women that a divorce was difficult to get and could cost

69

them in economic terms.[114] But there were limits to what she thought a wife should bear and that included wife-beating for which she advised legal separation[115] and, if necessary, police protection.[116] She owned that adultery could be a severe temptation for a woman caught in a stifling, loveless marriage but motherhood, "at once woman's glory and salvation," could be her redeeming comfort.[117]

At the time, motherhood was upheld as the ideal for all women and Kit was no exception. She told "Mary Lamb":

> ...don't you know that woman is very like to God—woman who is mother? We make the world, and we can unmake it. The maternal power is so vast, so infinite, far-reaching and enduring that in all the world of emotions, there is nothing to come near it. No woman has lived who has not been a mother. The beautiful suffering and yearning and patience of it! The pain and the joy![118]

Feminists who disagreed wrote to Kit, who berated them in return. She did not publish their letters but quoted passages that affronted her. "Independent" accused her of:

> "...lowering women by advising them to stop at home and not interest themselves in such great questions as those of temperance and lecturing against the iniquities of the world." She says she is "a woman's advocate" and as such she thinks it is her duty to "crush such women" as I am and to inform the community at large that the feminine sex "do not want babies." Poor woman and poorer babies!

The journalist went on to accuse such women as "Independent" of being willing to abandon any children they already had to illness, death or a life of crime as murderers.[119] Kit had a special place for letters from "cranks," as she called them. She threw them to a grinning devil doll, who sat on the rim of her wastebasket.[120]

Kit could protest as much as she liked, but, in reality, the romance of the motherhood image had its limits for many women. The birth rate in Canada was rapidly declining because of industrialization, which brought more women into the work force, compulsory education for children and strict child labour laws, making it more expensive to have children. Between 1871 and 1911, completed family size fell from 4.1 to 2.9 children, despite immigration. [121]

Clearly, birth control was being used, at least in middle-class families. In Canada, the usual methods were continence, prolonged nursing, coitus interruptus and abortion, which women believed was permissible until the third month, when the foetus quickened. To abort, they used drugs, potions, bleeding, vigorous exercise, gin, and dilation of the cervix with various appliances. Or they made a clandestine visit to a willing doctor or midwife. Abortion was illegal and so were birth control devices, such as rubbers, which were used by some couples. [122]

Many conservatives, appalled at the drop in the birth rate, blamed it partly on the "selfishness" of women who preferred independence to motherhood. But, as MacLaren and MacLaren point out:

> ...the decline in Canadian fertility was inextricably entangled in a web of sexual and social relationships...the doctors and priests, eugenicists and feminists, politicians and labour leaders who entered the discussion were far more concerned by the broader issues of sexual, social and political power than by the issue of family size. [123]

While individual journalists had their views on the issue, newspapers in general were essentially hypocritical in their treatment of birth control and abortion. Many, including the *Mail and Empire*, carried thinly disguised advertisements for birth control devices and abortificants, and at the same time, embroiled themselves in what was referred to as the "race suicide" issue in their news stories and editorials. [124]

Kit opposed both birth control and abortion. She considered motherhood a moral responsibility for all healthy women and simply could not understand why they would not want children. [125] Her sympathy could be aroused, however, by single women who found themselves pregnant and suicidal with nowhere to turn. One such woman was Jenny Newell, a domestic servant, who threw herself into the water at Niagara Falls, New York after her family and employer rejected her. She was rescued by a male passerby—whose heroism was given more media attention than her dilemma—and some time later gave birth to a healthy baby boy. [126]

Kit appealed for pity in cases such as this one, although she would never approve of abortion:

> We read of criminal operations in the papers and either blush or scowl—rarely do we tremble. Rarely do we realize the awful poignant affliction of the despairing one who sees no loophole but the awful ones of shame or death. Why aren't we decenter (sic) to one another, we women who suffer so? Why do we insist on giving our pity only when it is formally legalized by marriage? So many sad letters come to me. "What shall I do? He won't marry me nor dare I expect it. There is nothing but shame or the river. Oh! Kit, help!" God forgive men. They tempt us past belief and they are given to much backing out. [127]

At one point, well after her career was established, Kit, took on the medical establishment over the abortion issue. In March of 1908, the liberal Toronto *Sunday World*, a pre-dominantly working-class newspaper, quoted a crown attorney as saying that, for every local doctor caught performing abortions, fifty went free and so did 500 women who aborted themselves. Kit, who was more inclined to blame the doctors than the women, picked up the theme, declaring that there was a "formidable and shameful" list of such medical men, a contention that led to a skirmish with the editor of the *Canadian Practitioner*. He took her to task, claiming that all Toronto doctors, with the exception of half a dozen, were innocent. The journalist, unbowed, suggested that the local medical council and church leaders should show more muscle. [128]

In her rejection of sexual and political autonomy for women, and her support for equal pay and fair wages, Kit held contradictory views on women's rights. But that is not surprising given the times in which she lived and what we know of Kathleen's own history. She was a woman who had to make her own economic way in life—hence Kit's stance on equal pay and working conditions—but whose Irish,

Roman Catholic background may have made her reluctant
to publicly embrace the then radical causes of political and
sexual autonomy, especially in a conservative Canadian
society.

Kit's conflicting values resulted not only in her issuing
confusing sets of instructions to her female audience. They
affected her own literary ambitions, which reached far
beyond the woman's page. Professional and social constraints on her as a woman journalist dictated that she tend
the domestic side of both her public and private lives, but
in mid-career, she broke away from those confines and
tasted success. It was not as great as it might have been,
however, and her conflicts cost her.

Notes

1. *Daily Mail* 31 May 1890, 5.
2. Deborah Gorham, "Flora MacDonald Denison: Canadian Feminist," in L. Kealey, (ed.), *A Not Unreasonable Claim.*
3. *Andrew Rosen, Rise Up Women! The Militant Campaign of the Women's Social and Political Union 1903-1914* (London and Boston: Routledge and Kegan Paul 1974), 17.
4. Catherine L. Cleverdon, *The Woman Suffrage Movement in Canada*, Intro. Ramsay Cook (University of Toronto Press 1978), 4; in the United States, militancy was connected in the middle-class public mind with labour agitation. Eleanor Flexner, *Century of Struggle—the Woman's Rights Movement in the United States* (New York: Atheneum 1970), pp. 216-217.
5. Wendy Mitchinson "The WCTU: 'For God, Home and Native Land': A Study in Nineteenth-Century Feminism," in L. Kealey, (ed.), *A Not Unreasonable Claim*, 166.
6. Cleverdon, pp. 3-7.
7. Ibid., 20-26.
8. She did not specify which member had the problem. Response to "Total Abstainer," *Daily Mail*, 23 Jan 1892, 8.
9. Response to "Kingston Youth," Ibid., 27 Dec. 1890, 5.
10. About 25 per cent of Canada's suffrage leaders were writers and journalists, the largest identifiable group. Bacchi, 6.
11. *Daily Mail* 6 June 1891, 5. She made an exception in charity cases. Ibid., 4 July 1891, 5.
12. Ibid., 11 July 1891, 5.
13. The Sorosis Society was the first of the women's clubs in America. Marzolf, 22.
14. *New York Herald*, 14 June 1891, 9.
15. Ibid., 28 June 1891, 24. See also Ibid., 21 June 1891, 24. One of Watterson's freelance articles appeared under her byline in the Toronto *Globe*, 12 Dec. 1891, 11.
16. *Daily Mail*, 6 Jan. 1894, 5.
17. Toronto *Globe* 25 July 1891, 11; 19 Sept. 1891, 11. Her husband's biographer sees her as a liberal suffrage pioneer, but she was actually a conventional maternalist in much of her writing and not nearly as radical as some of her contemporaries. Harkness, pp. 16, 45.
18. See for example, Toronto *Empire*, 11 Feb. 1893, 7. Freeman was an active member of the Women's Christian Temperance Union. See the *Daily Mail*, 18 May 1893, 1.
19. Ibid., 21 May 1892, 5.

20. Ibid., 13 June 1890, 8; Bacchi, 66.
21. *Daily Mail*, 15 Oct. 1892, 4; 10 Oct. 1892, 8.
22. Machar in *Rose-Belford's Canadian Monthly National Review*, Vol. 2, June 1879, 675; Elliott in the Toronto *Globe*, 11, 18, 23 Apr. 1891, and 30 May 1891, 11; Duncan in *The Week*, 2 Dec. 1886.
23. Kit's equal pay sentiments are expressed briefly in her response to "Sam Jones" the same day. *Daily Mail*, 28 Mar. 1891, 5.
24. Ibid., 11 Apr. 1891, 5.
25. Eve Brodlique, who had covered Parliament Hill in Ottawa for the London, Ontario *Advertiser* in 1887 and 1888, eventually moved to Chicago. She blamed "lack of opportunity" in Canada for women's slow progress in the newspaper profession. She hoped newly established literary supplements would change the situation, although they were limiting. But the women "have accepted the limitation for the sake of the training." Quoted in "Women in Journalism," *The Week*, Vol. X, No. 30, (23 June 1893), 712.
26. Response to "A Little Miss," *Daily Mail*, 9 Aug. 1890, 8. A case in point is the advice book written several years later by E.A. Bennett, the editor of England's "Woman" magazine. His prose was littered with sarcastic complaints about women's poor grammar, worse spelling, general tardiness and lack of "business" sense. He warned them away from women's pages and papers, which he called "shameful" in their mediocrity, and told his readers to write "general" articles instead. E.A. Bennett, *Journalism for Women* (London and New York: John Lane 1898).
27. Response to "Anna S.," *Daily Mail*, 14 Nov. 1891, 9.
28. Response to "Bridget Malone," Ibid., 17 June 1893, 8. Even Sara Jeannette Duncan, who in many respects was more liberal than Kit, drew the line at reporting, believing that women could not think and write quickly or concisely enough to excel at it. "Bric-a-Brac," Montreal *Daily Star*, 25 Jan. 1888, n.p.
29. Response to "Edna," *Daily Mail*, 30 Aug. 1890, 8.
30. Ibid., 31 Jan. 1891, 8. Her comment may have been a reference to the case of Clara Brett Martin of Toronto, who fought and won for Canadian women the right to study and practice law. Cleverdon, 26; Bacchi, 15.
31. *Daily Mail*, 3 Oct. 1891, 11.
32. See Veronica Strong-Boag, "Canada's Women Doctors: Feminism Constrained," in L. Kealey, (ed.), *A Not Unreasonable Claim*.
33. *Daily Mail*, 31 Jan. 1891, 8. In a later series on careers for young people, the newspaper noted that most women physicians were working in hospitals or as missionaries, thereby presenting no competition to men in private practice. *Mail and Empire*, 19 May 1898, 6.

34. See Alison Prentice, "The Feminization of Teaching," in A. Prentice and S. Trofimenkoff, (eds.), *The Neglected Majority*, Vol. 1, (Toronto: McClelland and Stewart 1977); see also Judi Coburn, "'I See and Am Silent', A Short History of Nursing in Ontario," in J. Acton et al. (eds.), *Women at Work 1850-1930* (Toronto: Women's Press 1974).

35. *Mail and Empire*, 2 May 1896, 5.

36. *Daily Mail*, 3 Oct. 1891, 11.

37. Response to "S.H., Clinton," Ibid., 6 June 1891, 11.

38. Susan Strasser, *Never Done—The History of American Housework* (New York: Pantheon Books 1982), pp. 145-149.

39. In 1892, the average wage for this job was three dollars a week. Jean Thomson Scott, "The Conditions of Female Labour in Ontario," in W.J. Ashley, (ed.), *Toronto University Studies in Political Science*, First Series III (Toronto: Warwick and Sons 1892), 21.

40. *Daily Mail*, 12 April 1890, 5.

41. It was believed that prolonged standing could harm young women's health that way. Alice Klein and Wayne Roberts, "Besieged Innocence: The 'Problem' and Problems of Working Women— Toronto, 1896-1914," in J. Acton et al. (eds.), *Women at Work*.

42. *Daily Mail*, 16 May 1891, 5.

43. Ibid., 30 May 1891, 5. Shop girls made three to four dollars a week. Scott, "The Conditions of Female Labour in Ontario," 21.

44. Genevieve Leslie, "Domestic Service in Canada, 1880-1920," in J. Acton et al. (eds.), *Women at Work*, 72; Marilyn Barber, "Below Stairs: The Domestic Servant," in *Material History Bulletin*, 19, Ottawa, Spring 1984 (National Museum of Man), 38-40; Scott, "The Conditions of Female Labour in Ontario," pp. 19-20.

45. *Daily Mail*, 11 April 1891, 13.

46. The concern was expressed by businessmen and trade union leaders in particular, who were masking their real concern about the economic competition the women presented to men. Susan Mann Trofimenkoff, "A Hundred and Two Muffled Voices—Canada's Industrial Women in the 1880s," in *Atlantis*, Vol. 3, No. 1. Fall 1977, pp. 77-80.

47. Strasser, 6.

48. Jennifer Stoddard and Veronica Strong-Boag, "...And Things were Going Wrong at Home," in *Atlantis*, Vol. 1 No. 1. Fall 1975, 38.

49. Response to "May," *Daily Mail*, 31 Jan. 1891, 5.

50. Response to "J.A.N.," Ibid., 3 Sept. 1892, 6. See also the earlier response to the same reader who first wrote under the pen-name "Joanna." Ibid., 20 Aug. 1892, 8.

51. For example, the social gospel advocate, Agnes Maule Machar, who, while defending maids, tended to take a superior tone toward them. *The Week*, 6 Sept. 1895, 966; 27 Mar. 1896, 422.
52. Marilyn Barber, "The Women Ontario Welcomed: Immigrant Domestics for Ontario Homes, 1870-1930," in A. Prentice and S. Trofimenkoff (eds.), *The Neglected Majority*, Vol. II, (Toronto: McClelland and Stewart 1985), pp. 102-105.
53. *Daily Mail*, 14 Mar. 1891, 5.
54. Machar, *The Week*, 6 Sept. 1895, 966; 27 Mar. 1896, 422; Leslie, "Domestic Service in Canada 1880-1920," in J. Acton et al. (eds.), *Women at Work*, pp. 85-89.
55. *Daily Mail*, 10 Dec. 1892, 5. Barber explains that uniforms "eliminated any danger that the maid might be mistaken for the mistress and ensured that the neighbours and visitors would know that a maid was employed in the house." Barber, "Below Stairs," 43.
56. *Daily Mail*, 17 Dec. 1892, 8.
57. Ibid., 11 Jan. 1890, 5. Unmarried women of property had the municipal franchise in Toronto since 1884. Cleverdon, 22.
58. *Daily Mail*, 18 Jan. 1890, 5. See B.F. Austin, *Woman, Her Character, Culture and Calling* (Brantford, Ont: Book and Bible House 1890).
59. *Daily Mail*, 13 June 1890, 8; 14 June 1890, 10. Shaw was active in getting the Canadian suffrage movement established. Cleverdon, pp. 24-26.
60. When suffrage made the news pages, male reporters usually covered the story. Marzolf, 44.
61. *Daily Mail*, 21 June 1890, 5.
62. Ibid., 5 July 1890, 5.
63. See for example, Blakely Hall, "The Masculine Girl," in *Saturday Night*, 28 June 1890, 7.
64. Her question mark.
65. *Daily Mail*, 19 July 1890, 5.
66. Response to "Darwinian," Ibid., 25 Oct. 1890, 5.
67. Toronto *Globe*, 28 Feb. 1891, 11.
68. As "Garth Grafton." Ibid., 23 May 1885, 6. Duncan did not believe, however, that women knew enough about the law to become Members of Parliament. Ibid., 1 July 1885, 6.
69. Machar, in an early column cautiously signed "M", *Rose-Belford's Canadian Monthly and National Review*, Vol. 2, May 1879, pp. 568-579.
70. *Daily Mail*, 18 May 1893, 1.
71. Toronto *Empire*, 20 May 1893, 7.
72. *Daily Mail*, 29 Aug. 1891, 5; 4 Oct. 1890, 5.
73. See, for example, the editorial signed "T", *Saturday Night*, 7 June 1890, 1.

74. *Daily Mail*, 16 June 1890, 4; 18 Oct. 1890, 6.
75. Ibid., 9 May 1891, 6; see also 16, 23 May 1891, 6.
76. Ibid., 27 June 1891, 6.
77. Response to "Malcolm," Ibid., 12 Nov. 1892, 8. Years later, she described the funeral of an "old-fashioned" newspaper man, probably H.H. Wiltshire, who had recently died. "He liked women, but he only tolerated them. Always to him they were the inferior sex." "The Pedlar's Pack," *Canada Monthly*, May 1911, pp. 67-68. See also her response to "Old Reader" about the recent death of "The Flaneur," Hamilton *Herald*, 19 Aug. 1911, 8.
78. *Daily Mail*, 3 Sept. 1892, 5.
79. Ibid., 25 June 1892, 5.
80. Ibid., 7 June 1890, 5.
81. Ibid., 8 Nov. 1890, 5.
82. It was a common theme in advice books for and about adolescent girls. Gorham, *The Victorian Girl*, pp. 101-102.
83. Response to "Chatterbox," *Daily Mail*, 14 June 1890, 5.
84. Ibid., 23 May 1891, 5.
85. Ibid., 6 June 1891, 5.
86. Ibid., 29 Nov. 1890, 5.
87. Linda Gordon, *Woman's Body, Woman's Right—A Social History of Birth Control in America* (New York: Penguin Books, 1977), pp. 116-120.
88. Writer's question mark. *Daily Mail*, 20 Dec. 1890, 5.
89. Gorham, *The Victorian Girl*, 117.
90. *Daily Mail*, 20 Dec. 1890, 5.
91. Ibid., 4 Apr. 1891, 5.
92. Ibid., 7 Nov. 1891, 5.
93. Response to "Monica," Ibid., 24 Jan. 1891, 5. See also 20 June 1891, 5.
94. Gorham, *The Victorian Girl*, pp. 90-91.
95. *Daily Mail*, 24 Feb. 1894, 5.
96. Ibid., 16 May 1891, 5; 14 July 1891, 5.
97. Ibid., 11 Apr. 1891, 5.
98. Responses to "Edith" and "Perplexity," Ibid., 31 May 1890, 5.
99. Ibid., 14 May 1892, 8.
100. Ibid., 25 Sept. 1891, 5.
101. Ibid., 20 Aug. 1892, 5. See also her response to "Merry Sunshine," and the letter from "A Woman," who cheered her on. Ibid., 3 Sept. 1892, 6; Ibid., 1 Oct. 1892, 6.
102. Ibid., 18 July 1891, 5.
103. Ibid., 22 Aug. 1891, 5.
104. Ibid., 12 Sept. 1891, 5.
105. Ibid., 24 Sept. 1892, pp. 5-6.

106. Response to "Senorita," Ibid., 22 Oct. 1892, 8.
107. Response to "Caesar," Ibid., 10 June 1893, 8.
108. Ibid., 29 Oct. 1892, 8.
109. Responses to "Lizzie Hexam," "Jay Kay," and "St. George, (Victoria, B.C.)," Ibid., 3 Dec. 1892, 8; response to "Que Vive," 10 Dec. 1892, 8.
110. Ibid., 19 Nov. 1892, 8.
111. Ibid., 22 Apr. 1893, 5.
112. Ibid., 24 Feb. 1894, 5. In response, two horrified readers accused her of encouraging maids to leave domestic service and housewives to become idle society women. Ibid., 17 Mar. 1894, 5.
113. Ibid., 16 July 1892, 5.
114. Ibid., 8 Oct. 1892, 5. One could get a divorce only through a private Member's bill in Parliament. The process cost one thousand dollars or more and took a year. Adultery was the usual grounds. Gary Kinsman, *The Regulation of Desire—Sexuality in Canada* (Montreal: Black Rose Books 1987), pp. 85-86.
115. Response to "A Miserable Woman," *Mail and Empire*, 17 Aug. 1895, 6.
116. Ibid., 30 May 1896, 5.
117. Ibid., 29 Jan. 1898, Part 2, 4. She received many letters in praise of this essay. Ibid., 12 Feb. 1898, Part 2, 4.
118. Ibid., 29 Feb. 1896, 6.
119. *Daily Mail*, 3 Jan. 1891, 9.
120. Ibid., 16 May 1891, 11.
121. Angus MacLaren and Arlene Tigar MacLaren, *The Bedroom and the State* (Toronto: McClelland and Stewart 1986), pp. 11-21.
122. Ibid., Chapter 2.
123. Ibid., 10.
124. For example, the *Mail and Empire* carried such ads on several pages. *Mail and Empire*, 21 Mar. 1908. For a critical look at the role of North American newspapers in the abortion issue, written from an anti-abortion point of view, see Marvin N. Olasky, *The Press and Abortion 1838-1988* (Hillsdale, N.J: Erlbaum Publishers, 1988).
125. Response to "Pansy Blossom," *Daily Mail*, 14 Mar. 1891, 5; response to "L.O.," *Mail and Empire*, 17 Dec. 1898, Part 2, 4.
126. *Daily Mail*, 30 May 1893, 3.
127. *Mail and Empire*, 17 Aug. 1895, 5.
128. Ibid., 21 Mar. 1908, 21; 4 Apr. 1908, 21.

Kit explores the seamier side of London.
(From the Toronto *Daily Mail* 1892.)

CHAPTER 3
ADVENTURER OR MOTHER?

In 1892, two years after Kit joined the *Mail*, she became a travel writer, producing articles primarily for the "Kingdom," which she conducted at long distance through the mail. Travel articles had great popular appeal as they represented adventure to a nineteenth century audience. Those readers who could not afford to go on long trips themselves could partake in the adventures of writers and journalists such as Kit, who were expected to relay home vivid and descriptive narratives of their experiences.[1] Female and male travel writers used a great deal of colour and literary license; for example, satire of a particular person met on one's travels, rather than analytic pieces on a country or its mores, was a favorite method of conveying information.[2] The technique resulted in what Eva-Marie Kroller calls "multifaceted fragments rather than lengthy narratives embodying a centralist world view."[3]

In 1892, with "Theodocia" as a travelling companion,[4] Kit visited her home in Ireland, went on to Paris and then to England, where she wrote a well-received series on Charles Dickens' London. The articles brought her descriptive writing talents into the limelight and underlined her concern for the less fortunate.[5]

The 1890s was the era of "stunt" journalism in the newspaper world. An adventurous journalist would become the main participant in an exciting exploit and then write about the experience. One of the most famous instances was the 1889 journey of Elizabeth Cochrane ("Nelly Bly") of the New York *World* around the world in 72 days.[6]

Much of Kit's material was gathered during several late nights when, daringly dressed as a man[7] but safely in the company of a male detective, she ventured into "all sorts of queer places, thieves' kitchens, tramps' shelters, midnight markets, Jews' corners and other savory spots."[8] Her descriptions of her wanderings through the seedier parts of the city—especially the neighborhoods along the bank of the River Thames—could be lurid:

> Butchers' boys, in playful endeavours to hit some other lads down the lane, let fly a bit of tainted meat that strikes you under the ear, and cats prowl among the dirty fish stalls, and small, lean dogs, generally of a whitey brown appearance and character, growl at one another in the sawdust under the butchers' stalls. If Noah Claypole went on the "kinchin' lay" about this neighbourhood, he would do a famous business, for everywhere, small girls with big pitchers are going to and from public houses with coppers clenched tightly in their cold, red fingers... We reach Limehouse Church at last, and go into the mortuary and look at "Found Drowned" and others laid out on slabs like fish, waiting to be identified and buried. Not a pleasant sight, these poor dead creatures whom nobody seems to care enough to make enquiries about..."[9]

In these articles, Kit's social concerns overshadowed her attempts at literary entertainment. The squalor that she witnessed in her two months of wandering in the city set her off in an angry tirade against the privileged:

> ...the "classes," forsooth! who look on the "masses" as the human carpet over which they can tread at their leisure in their pursuit after wealth, and all that tends to feed every sensual and gross appetite, every coarse feeling. I suppose I shouldn't talk this way, dear girls, but indeed, if you were here, and wandering as I am here and there from the great West End to the filthy squalid dens of the very poor, your hearts would feel sore—sore.[10]

She deflected any criticism of her point of view with an impassioned defense of the work of Charles Dickens, who "taught us to look around and see the misery and distress lying at our doors..."[11] Kroller criticizes Kit, however, as being too quick to draw her readers' attention to reassuring symbols of British Empire, such as Westminster Abbey, "in keeping with her double (even duplicitous) function as social critic and spokesman for an official organ."[12]

The London series was colourful and imaginative— although perhaps not strictly factual—and was well-received by the public and Kit's newspaper colleagues. One unnamed London *Times* journalist wrote to "The "Flaneur" that he and other British newspapermen had noted the series with much interest: "The *Daily Mail* is fortunate to have on its staff one of the smartest women writers in America."[13]

For the next three years Kit travelled widely, writing vivid articles about the places and people she visited. Her travels allowed her to appeal to a wide audience—a fact of which she was well aware—and she avoided writing about events of primary interest to women. Her coverage of the 1893 Chicago World Fair was a case in point.

It was one of her major trips away from Toronto, during which she was expected to produce the descriptive, imaginative kind of writing she had done in London. At first, Kit was overwhelmed by the sight of the "White City":

> ...the gathered art of centuries, the rich stuffs of Eastern bazaars, the paintings, sculptures, inventions, curios of ages and ages are laid open to your amazed eyes, and there is so much to be seen and studied and learned in this huge city of treasures that you feel that time is too short, that you are physically too feeble, mentally too puny to take in half the beauty and knowledge that lie stretched out before you in those long lines of graceful white buildings...[14]

She spent several weeks wandering around the Fair, investigating the various buildings and the "villages" where peoples of other countries had set up their displays. In her attempt to make the foreign not just interesting but familiar, Kit appealed to universal maternalism in her account of a brief meeting she had with a woman from Java:

> She wore a loose jacket of yellow silk, and a petticoat of red
> stuff, wound around her figure Japanese fashion, that is,
> without "gathers" or any kind of fulness (sic). In her ears
> were huge round earrings like coat buttons, and when she
> pulled one out and handed it to us to look at, the hole in her
> lobe was large enough to admit the little finger. Her shapely
> brown legs and feet were bare, and her black hair was twisted
> in a loose knot high on her head. On each arm there were
> from four to six bangles and her brown hands were soft and
> small. "You lost your baby, didn't you?" I said to the little
> brown woman. She understood. A queer change came over
> her pretty face. Her big eyes, always sad, grew more mourn-
> ful and with a clap of her hands, she ran into her little bamboo
> house. We heard her moaning there, and watched her from
> the doorway, sitting on her dusky heels and rocking herself
> to and fro. Poor little brown woman! I was sorry I spoke. [15]

The incident fell far short of the opportunities available
to her to report on women's concerns. During the week of
May 20-27 1893, a Women's Congress of notable feminists,
professionals, club women and others, had met at the Fair
to discuss women's rights and other issues. But the *Daily
Mail* paid this event little attention, despite the presence of
a Canadian delegation, [16] and Kit merely wasn't sent to
Chicago until well after the Congress was over. Political
debates still took place in the Women's Building over the
summer, however, but the journalist usually busied herself
elsewhere on the fair site. The exception was her reverent
treatment of the display on literary women which included
the portraits and manuscripts of George Eliot, Jane Austen
and Charlotte Bronte:

> And they are all here—the holy things, and you go down
> on your knees in the great room upstairs—the great room
> with the painted ceiling...and you forget all about the other
> women and the frou frou of silk, and the pleasant murmur
> of women's voices, and the whole of it, because you are
> staring—in your short-sighted way, with your nose flattened
> against the glass, and your hat anywhere—into a case and
> in at the written lines of Adam Bede. [17]

Kit, referring to many of the Women's Building exhibits,
explained that she wasn't really that interested in needle-

work and found it difficult to write about for that reason.[18] In the one column in which she did mention the women's political debates—exercises apparently vigorous enough to offend her genteel sense of ladylike decorum—she had a fit of bad temper. She described the Women's Building as "...a hideous, square old thing, with horrid horned and winged nonentities sticking out of it, like abnormal ears" and the debates as "hysterical":

> In this delightful hen roost the hens all cackle together. It is "sit down" and "get out!" and "Be decent whatever you are!" (reminding one of Sairey Gamp and Drink Fair) and its blows with the handles of parasols, and flushings, and tears, and hysterics. "Mothers of motions" don't know what to do with their offspring, and seconders of resolutions are told to "shut up." And the male world chuckles. It is a pity that a few crowing hens should drown the gentle cackling of the others, who really are doing no harm at all. It's your tiny bantam lady who makes all the noise, while your great Cochin Chinas and featherlegged Brahmas snuggle their heads in their necks, and go to sleep until it's all over.[19]

Kit insisted to her readers that women were interested in far more than the "general ravings of the descent of man or ascent of woman" and, to illustrate, wrote a detailed essay on the construction of a canal in Chicago. She declared that such a topic should interest women because, being far more intelligent than given credit for, they wanted to be better companions to their husbands and better mothers to their children.[20]

The journalist stayed in Chicago for several months, occasionally venturing out of her small, untidy room, which was littered with paper and books,[21] in search of more adventure. Several times, she gained access to all-male bastions frequented by newspapermen. Such an august establishment was the Whitechapel Club, devoted to its absentee "president," Jack the Ripper, and furnished with macabre relics and photographs of famous murders. Kit hinted broadly that she gained entrance secretly, and whether she was "arrayed in the insignia of my sex or not it is not my purpose to state."[22] She also paid a visit to the all-male

Chicago Press Club. She was treated politely as a woman, but felt like an outsider. Still, she wasn't sure that female journalists were comfortable enough with each other to form their own clubs. [23]

Kit's letters from Chicago were well received by most of her readers, but not all of them were happy about the way she handled the assignment. She was quick to defend herself, however, explaining that some of her letters were never published because they were "crowded out" by other material chosen by the editors of the *Mail*. [24] She soon found herself off on another odyssey, one that took her away from Toronto for the better part of a year.

In March 1894, she left for the California Mid-winter Fair in San Francisco, where she repeated her "stunt journalism" techniques, such as touring the opium dens of Chinatown at night, dressed as a man and with a detective in tow. [25] Writing from San Jose in June, she described how she coped with a travel writer's life:

> Just now I am writing the Kingdoms in all sorts of places—on steamboats, in woods and gardens, and in queer little top rooms on twelve-inch rickety tables. Last week I wrote on a band box. [26]

She would also see New Mexico, British Columbia, the Rockies, Quebec City, the Maritimes and the West Indies with a two-month stopover in Toronto to break up her tour. She did not go home for Christmas. Writing from Baddeck, Nova Scotia, she told her readers she was about to take a boat to Jamaica and Barbados even though, by this time she was feeling "tired and homeless sometimes." [27] But her articles were earning her an international reputation. *America's Greatest Men and Women* said:

> Certainly no other woman on the continent, and possibly no man below the rank of editor-in-chief, exercises so direct an influence upon the prestige and circulation of a newspaper as does Mrs. Kathleen Blake Watkins of the Toronto *Mail*. By her brilliant work, Mrs. Watkins has made a splendid reputation for that journal and for herself. [28]

Kathleen Blake Coleman's children, "Patsy" and "Thady," ca. 1894.
(Courtesy of Mrs. Kit Waterous)

But, despite the fact that her Canadian audience enjoyed her travel work,[29] Kit's roaming days were numbered, at least for awhile. In February 1895, the *Daily Mail* merged with the *Empire*. Kit stayed on as the women's page editor[30] with potentially twice as many readers as she had before.[31] It soon became evident, however, that, with the exception of short trips to nearby communities and cities, her newspaper was no longer willing to let her travel.[32] Kit abandoned her adventuresome side and placed a new emphasis on the maternal, introducing her real-life children and adored household pets into the "Kingdom."

J.V. MacAree, one of her colleagues on the *Mail and Empire*, later wrote that it was unusual for a journalist to discuss his or her private life the way Kit did in her columns: "...in the era of a more reticent and formal journalism they were almost epoch-making, and gave her early distinction."[33] It is not clear exactly why she took the risk. It may have been a response to the conservatism of the *Mail and Empire*, which may have wanted her to be more "womanly," or a way of keeping old readers and attracting new ones. Kathleen's private papers hold an interesting clue: they suggest that by the mid-'90s, perhaps as a response to her fame, the distinction between her private and public personalities was becoming blurred. From San Francisco, she had sent home a photograph of herself inscribed: "To my two dear children—Teddy and Kathleen—from their loving mother. Kit."[34]

Many of her stories about "Thady" and "Patsey"[35] were apparently based on real incidents. From what she wrote of them, they gave her much emotional support. After work, Thady always waited for her arrival on the six o'clock tram and greeted her by taking her satchel and throwing an affectionate arm around her.[36] When she was ill, both children nursed her.[37] In one humorous episode, they helped their frightened mother catch a mouse[38] and, in another, laced with pathos, all three mourned the death of the family dog.[39] The children were Kit's companions, especially Thady, with whom she loved playing pranks, once hiding in the woods with him and throwing chestnuts at an irate male passerby.[40] Christmases were the happiest times:

> The dearest gifts I got were a small square of linen worked in yellow and white floss with "Mother" worked bravely across the centre, the first bit of needle work done by the dear stumbling child-fingers, and, a student's shade for the eyes which a thoughtful lad had searched many a store for.[41]

Stories and comments about her children allowed her to fill the "Kingdom" every week with material designed to entertain and touch her readers and give her additional authority as a maternal advisor. Kit believed that, because mothers were often guilty of "overpetting" their sons, boys should be sent away to school to learn how to be men. Without naming names, she wrote about one difficult farewell:

> His small heart is full to bursting. You who know him as no other woman in all the world can ever know him, read his grief and his love in his large, soft eyes, that at times take on the gentleness of a girl's. He is bearing up bravely and you are fighting with a queer thing in your throat.[42]

Her relationship with her daughter was different. Kit imbued boys with superiority by virtue of their gender; daughters were more fragile.

> It is a great thing to be the mother of a man. And, too, perhaps, a lurking thought of the pain life brings to a woman makes her a little sorry when a girl baby is born. She cries softly in the night over the little face that lies so near her heart. No matter what good luck may come to her, there must be moments of suffering in her girl's life which can never touch her boy's.

A mother loved her son and daughter equally but "the girl has more of the protecting love perhaps. The boy more of the proud and passionate love."[43] When accused of favouring her son over her daughter, she angrily replied:

> My Patsy is the dearest, wisest, sweetest being living, as she well knows, very dear to her mother indeed. I would not have you or anyone think that the one child is dearer to me than the other.[44]

89

The inclusion of the children in the "Kingdom" certainly threatened the family's privacy. Sometimes readers presumed to tell Kit how to raise her children, advice which she did not welcome. She sarcastically thanked "Earthy", who advised her to buy a house, get a housekeeper and send the children to public schools[45] and vehemently denied the accusation of "A Mother's Friend" that she exploited her children by writing about them. She claimed that they did not read her columns and were not concerned about what appeared in the "Kingdom".[46] It was a "delight" for her to be able to write about her children and, although she worried about boring her readers, she felt it brought her closer to the mothers among them "in the shadowy way I like best." She felt they could relate to her stories[47] and many did. She received numerous Christmas greetings for the children[48] and some readers even dedicated verses to them, which she passed on to the editor of another *Mail and Empire* Saturday feature, "The Children's Corner."[49]

In the meantime, she skirmished with the new management of the *Mail and Empire* over the contents of her women's page, with Kit insisting on keeping its intellectual content. Tongue-in-cheek, she introduced a male voice, "Autocylus" with his "Pedlar's Pack" of various topics that supposedly only men could talk about. His interests and style of writing were so similar to Kit's own that it is obvious he was her invention and, after a few weeks, his presence was apparently considered unnecessary and he disappeared.[50]

The *Mail and Empire* then introduced two new women's features consisting of material Kit avoided. They were a fashion page with lavish illustrations and material taken from other publications[51] and a daily column, "For and About Women," which, Kit assured her readers, was not written by her and was "none of my concern."[52] The column included news of many different kinds of women's clubs and organizations, such as the YWCA's regular monthly meeting and the WCTU's mock "Parliament of Women."[53]

It also featured household hints and simplistic advice on pleasing one's husband, which Kit roundly criticized.[54]

For her part, she preferred to discuss economics, literature and politics. She won her point, despite opposition from some of her readers and her editor. For example, she advised women on how to invest in gold stocks, resulting (*writing*) in criticism from businessmen and praise from readers impressed with her knowledge.[55] Despite the fact that the *Mail and Empire* already had a literary page, she continued to review those books she found interesting after her readers took her side. She gloated about her victory over the editor. "I am crowing out loud though I know the penalties attached to the crowing hen."[56]

Another of her favourite topics was politics. Although the *Mail and Empire* was firmly Conservative, Kit did not, at first, take a strong party line. She identified herself as a liberal writer on a Conservative organ who insisted on adhering to her broad-minded philosophies.[57] At the time, for example, President Cleveland of the United States was threatening to invoke the Monroe Doctrine and confiscate non-American possessions in North America, leading to Canadian fears of war with its southern neighbour.[58] In January, 1896, Kit and other women journalists visited the House of Commons in Ottawa, where she modestly wrote "From A Woman's Standpoint," that, with the American threat, it was time for closer ties with Britain and solidarity on federal-provincial relations, which she placed ahead of the particularly vexing problem of the Manitoba School question.

> Turn to the Dominion policy of building on and perfecting by closer communication with England. British capital ought to be pouring in here now, where there is no fear of confiscation, if you will only strike while the iron is hot and drop the party question of education and pause before entering on provincial quarrels, entailing further stops and further delays.[59]

Kit described her frank impressions of the House, and of several politicians, including Wilfrid Laurier. She found he

91

had a "face full of tact but lacking in power...smiling and
bland" but sensed his real strength and was puzzled: "What
then, is Mr. Laurier a living Paradox?"[60] He was elected
Prime Minister that year and was soon to become her friend.
From the evidence in her private papers, Kathleen used her
connections with him to try to further her career, particularly during her next major journey.

Kit had been feeling restricted in her movements and had
continued to fight for the chance to travel again. An
unsigned poem which appeared on her page early in 1896
testified to her extreme restlessness: "You have tied me
down to the desk and the pen. The hurrying pen all day
..."[61] and she urged her readers to write to the editor if "you
want Kit to take trips."[62] But their support was apparently
not enough to persuade management. If the journalist was
to take another long journey, it would be one which would
be money well spent and a boost to the circulation of the
Mail and Empire. Her opportunity came in the summer of
1897 when she was sent to London, England to cover Queen
Victoria's Diamond Jubilee. This time, Thady went with her.

Her descriptions of the Jubilee celebrations, with their
pomp and pageantry, earned a more prominent place in the
Mail and Empire than her usual efforts for the "Kingdom."
Her three-page description of the motherly Queen, her regal
procession and the accompanying military ceremonies must
have strongly appealed to the pro-Monarchist sentiments
of her audience:

> This woman, sitting in the open carriage within hand-reach
> of her people, surrounded by no guards, knowing well that
> she need no "protection" from the crowd that adored her,
> expressed in all her attitude that of mother more than any-
> thing else. Right and left she bowed, smiling very little, and
> bowing oftenest to the poorer people on the edge of the pave-
> ment...Suddenly the immense mass of people began to chant
> the National Anthem. It was a mighty moment.[63]

To do her assignments well, Kathleen apparently used
her professional prominence and any social connections she
had. Prime Minister Laurier, who was also in London for

the Jubilee, assured her that he would help her if he could.[64] A month later, when he invited Kit to accompany him and Mrs. Laurier to Buckingham Palace to see the Prince of Wales present medals to the Colonial troops, her story made the front page of the *Mail and Empire's* features section.[65]

From London, Kit and Thady went on to Ireland. Again, she was on assignment, covering a tour of the Duke and Duchess of York[66] for both the *Mail and Empire* and for a prominent London newspaper, the *Daily Mail*, for which she had been freelancing.[67] In the meantime, Prime Minister Laurier smoothed the way for her by sending a letter introducing her to a Major Streathfield, Commander of the Forces office in Dublin:

> Mrs. Watkins is a lady of unique culture and intelligence; she is well known in the best circles of Canadian society, and I will be responsible that in assisting her, your confidence will be entirely well placed.[68]

Kathleen may have been hoping that her work in London and Ireland would lead to greater things. At some point, she and Laurier discussed some "scheme" that involved a job for her in England—perhaps even a permanent one—but nothing came of it.[69]

On her return to Canada, Kit fulfilled her dream of publishing a book, *To London for the Jubilee*, which consisted of her newspaper columns from her trip.[70] In the "Kingdom," she shamelessly plugged the seventy-five-cent publication as a Christmas gift.[71] Her reaction to her book was an odd mixture of elation and disappointment:

> I got such a fit of childishness—I think I'll call it—when I saw myself up on a poster—my pen-name I mean—in the booksellers' windows. I wanted Thady that minute to throw up his cap and stand on his head. Its my first bit of a book, you know, and I feel like an old child who has got a penny doll too late and had forgotten how to play with it.[72]

Despite the *Mail and Empire's* advertising claims,[73] the book did not sell well.[74] Reviewers were enthusiastic, however, and Kit became even more well known.[75]

But journalistic success was not enough. Despite her adventures and the praise and recognition she received, Kit had been depressed, on and off, for years. She had occasionally considered suicide[76] but managed to struggle through her difficult times by seeking solace from nature, where she found God.[77]

The main reason for her unhappiness was her deep sense of failure in never fulfilling her ambition to become a leading literary light. She was unable to achieve what she might have, partly because she lacked confidence in her talents. She gradually realized that to earn her living as a journalist and become a successful writer at the same time was an impossible task.

In order to pursue her literary goals, Kit needed male inspiration and approval. She had entertained high hopes for her series about Dickens' London and wanted to publish it in book form.[78] But just at that point, her beloved father, for whom the series was written, died. He had, she wrote, inspired her with "the love that is the most glorious incentive in the world," but he never saw the London letters and his death affected her shaky confidence in their literary worth. "After (he died) Dickens fell flat, and the letters were poor, and bald, and since—well, one loses heart."[79]

Her readers urged her to publish a book about the Chicago World Fair but she was not sure that, as "an obscure journalist," she could compete with the work of established male writers who had also written about the event. She felt intimidated and unsure of herself. "I fear the hopelessness that failure would bring."[80] Even her extensive travels in 1894 did little to bolster her confidence. She harboured an acute sense of inadequacy because she was a newspaperwoman, not a female literary star.

> ...the mediocre success we, alas! most of us arrive at, is almost more fatal than utter failure. I often think this, scribbling as I do, every week in more or less failing fashion, and I do tell you that often the thought is heart-breaking. This drifting failure, this shallow incompetency. Sometimes one wonders is it the lot of women? But then come the beacon-lights—Eliot,

Humphrey Ward, Georges Sand—clarion calls, the very
names of them are; and we respond, we weaker ones, and
shrill feebly that we are coming—we are coming.[81]

At times, she lost all hope of ever achieving her literary
ambitions, believing that she was destined to remain a
women's page editor. Gloomily, she recollected her early
days in journalism when she was fired with a desire for fame
and "that first 'KIT' in print was such a wonder of golden
letters, so large that they spread over the whole page." But
six years as a journalist had taught her that fame did not
come easily "and the letters in 'Kit' have dwindled down
to ink dots." She believed she had found her own level in
the newspaper world,[82] and anyway, her job on the *Mail and
Empire* was so demanding that she did not have the time to
write anything else. "If you have certain matter to bring out
every week, and a space of six or seven columns to fill, it
wears on you so that your other work—on magazine or
novel—is killed."[83]

As it was, she was sometimes overwhelmed by the
amount of work she had to do just to keep the "Kingdom"
going, so much so that it threatened her health. After she
returned from her travels in 1895, she became ill for several
weeks, seriously enough to feel that she was "wasting
away."[84] On several occasions, she "faked" some of her
material to help her through illnesses or absences; for example, during the month of October 1897, the *Mail and Empire*
re-ran a few of her old columns and answers, some altered
slightly to make it look as if they were fresh.[85] The pressure
of deadlines was sometimes overwhelming: "Sometimes I
feel that I must sit on Time, and hold him down while I get
a few extra strokes of the pen; but he always bobs up
serenely and ticks away at the top of my desk in a cruelly
triumphant manner," she once wrote.[86]

Kit never discussed any feelings she might have had over
spending months away from her children because of her
work. But given that she wrote of them with love and
pride—and that she was well aware of the contemporary

95

attitudes towards motherhood—she would have found it impossible not to feel guilty.

Certainly her professional ambitions and the demands of her job seemed to conflict with her desire for an intimate relationship. Around the time she and E.J. Watkins split up, and shortly after her successful trip to London, an unsigned poem appeared in the "Kingdom." It testified to a struggle for the heart of the writer between Love, Fame and Death— with Death the eventual victor.

> My heart a cemetery is, wherein
> Three furtive phantoms ceaselessly unite,
> And toss the gauntlet, and prepare each night
> To battle each with each till one shall win.
> Beautiful as an uncommitted sin
> Is one, with but an arrowed bow bedight;
> And one is armed in flame, and mailed in light
> The third bears the swift scythe, curved keen and thin.
> The restless combat for my heart, their prey
> Began long years ago, yet still they brawl,
> Though Love—the first dear phantom—faints for breath
> And soon will falter, weary of the fray;
> Then Fame will drop the sword, and both will fall
> And leave the triple victory to Death![87]

Kit's work left her little time for a private life, and she was lonely. After "Theodocia" left her columns, she lived in a boarding house with "Patsy Brannigan," her pet rat, who was her only company.[88] She later recalled that she was often kept awake at night by the neighbours' crying children or various musical instruments and had to put up with inferior food and a grouchy landlady.[89] In short, she led:

> ...a restless, comfortless, homeless life—full of hard work, with never a home circle—never a place but a desolate room in some business block to go to, and many private troubles besides and scanty means.[90]

At this point, she told one of her readers that she did not believe in love between the sexes any more. "As far as I am concerned the thing was worn threadbare ages ago, and thrown away like a shabby coat. Let's not talk about it."[91] Her closest friend then was a woman she loved "better than

96

I loved any man, or ever will."[92] She did not often get to see the "Scotch-Canadian," but shared with her, nonetheless, a "very green and very tender" love.[93] The woman was probably Jean Blewett, the new women's page editor of the Toronto *Globe*, whose main claim to fame was her popular, sentimental poems about every-day occurences.[94] The two women became fast friends, often lauding each other in print.[95]

In 1895, after her seven-week illness brought on by over-work, Kit published another unsigned poem, which spoke of tiredness with life and the absence "of sweet caringness to heal Love's smart."[96] She later advised a would-be journalist, who was happily married but bored at home, to count her blessings:

> If you only knew what that "happy at home" means to the women who are out fighting for the children's bread! taking the place of men and yet feeling utterly feminine, so longing to have someone to care and to help and to shelter. Stay at home, little woman.[97]

In 1898, Kit was handed two opportunities that might have solved both her professional lack of confidence and her personal loneliness. First of all, she was offered the assignment that has made her famous—the Spanish-American War in Cuba. It was not, however, the triumph she hoped it would be or that legend has made it. She was also offered the love of a good man. Both events meant she had to reassess what she wanted from her life.

Notes

1. Most travelling journalists were subsidized by their newspapers and their subscribers. Steamship fare across the Atlantic cost between $130 and $150. Eva-Marie Kroller, *The Canadian Traveller in Europe 1851-1900* (Vancouver: University of British Columbia Press 1987), pp. 28, 59. Kit did not live extravagantly on the road. In London, she rented a cold attic room in a small hotel or boarding house where "a little demon of a wind" blew the snow around her windows. Response to "Merry Sunshine," *Daily Mail*, 26 Mar. 26, 1892, 6; response to "Rick," Ibid., 16 Apr. 1892, 6.

2. See, for example, Grace Denison, *A Happy Holiday* (Toronto: Grace E. Denison 1890) and Sara Jeannette Duncan, *A Social Departure: How Orthodocia and I Went Round the World By Ourselves* (New York: Appleton 1890).

3. Kroller, pp. 7, 105-106.

4. Women travelling alone were considered daring and not quite respectable. Ibid., 74.

5. "Tramps with the Genius of London," *Daily Mail*, 12 Mar.-16 April 1892, 5.

6. Cochrane's best journalism was the investigative work she did after she returned from her travels. Marzolf, 23.

7. The literary historian Jeannette Foster notes that the cross-dressed woman has been a literary motif since ancient times, but in the late nineteenth century, with the advent of sexologists such as Havelock Ellis, such a woman would be understood to be rebelling against the feminine role and might be suspected of lesbianism. Jeannette Foster, *Sex Variant Women in Literature* (Vantage Press 1956, repr. Tallahassee, Fla.: The Naiad Press Inc. 1985), especially Chapters I and IV.

8. Response to "Rosalind," *Daily Mail*, 11 June 1892, 5. Her physical size probably helped her disguise. She was slim and stood over five-feet-seven-inches. Response to "Chipit," *Mail and Empire*, 25 Apr. 1896, 5.

9. *Daily Mail*, 2 Apr. 1892, 5. In *Oliver Twist*, the villain Fagin discusses the "kinchin lay"—the practice of stealing money from children who were on errands—with Noah Claypole, the former charity-boy he hires. Charles Dickens, *Oliver Twist*. Intro. Humphrey House (New York and Toronto: Oxford University Press 1970), 325.

10. *Daily Mail*, 9 Apr. 1892, 6.

11. Ibid., 16 Apr. 1892, 5.

12. Kroller, pp. 121-122.

13. *Daily Mail*, Saturday Supplement, 25 June 1892, 1.

14. Ibid., 29 July, 1893, 5.
15. Ibid.
16. A short article about them appeared in the *Daily Mail*, 18 May 1893, 1. In contrast both the Toronto *Globe* and the Toronto *World* gave some of the congress front page coverage. Toronto *World*, 18 May 1893, 1; Toronto *Globe*, 20 May 1893, 1. Additional coverage to the *Globe* was provided by its own woman's page editor, Mrs. Willoughby Cummings ("SAMA"). Cummings, a leader of the Anglican Woman's Auxiliary, successfully used her position as a journalist and congress delegate to organize a Canadian branch of the International Council of Women. Veronica Strong-Boag, *Parliament of Women: The National Council of Women of Canada 1893-1919* (Ottawa: National Museums of Canada 1976), pp. 73-75; Toronto *Globe*, 27 May 1893, 16. Alice Fenton Freeman ("Faith Fenton") covered the congress for the Toronto *Empire*. See, for example, Toronto *Empire*, 20 May 1893, 7.
17. *Daily Mail*, 7 Oct. 1893, 5.
18. Ibid., 30 Sept. 1893, 5.
19. Ibid., 19 Aug. 1893, 5.
20. Ibid., 2 Dec. 1893, 5.
21. Response to "Bede," Ibid., 28 Oct. 1893, 8.
22. Schudson describes the Whitechapel Club as a place where (male) journalists gathered to talk "shop" and criticize each others' work. Schudson, 69.
23. *Daily Mail*, 23 Dec. 1893, 5. In fact, they had been doing so in the United States since the mid-1880s. Marzolf, 26.
24. Response to "9th Dec.," *Daily Mail*, 16 Dec. 1893, 8.
25. Ibid., 21 June 1894, 5; *Mail and Empire*, 17 Aug. 1895, 5.
26. Response to "A Woman of No Importance," *Daily Mail*, 16 June 1894, 5.
27. Response to "Sad Sack," Ibid., 8 Dec. 1894, 5.
28. Vol. 2, No. 8, 12 May 1894, 122. Clipping in PAC K.B.C. Papers, Vol. 4, File 1. See also the various clippings in her scrapbook. Vol. 3, File 1.
29. Response to "Elizabeth," *Daily Mail*, 8 Dec. 1894, 5; letter from "A Fermanagh Irishman," *Mail and Empire*, 13 Apr. 1895, 5.
30. Alice Fenton Freeman ("Faith Fenton") lost her job as women's page editor of the *Empire* in the merger. Kit later wrote that Freeman's page in the *Empire* was "one of the brightest, tenderest, most sympathetic pages ever written by any woman." Vancouver *News Advertiser*, 16 Nov. 1913, 10.
31. An editorial on the day the merger took effect said the *Daily Mail* effectively doubled its circulation. The merger was an effort to cut down on what was described as "unhealthy competition" among

newspapers; that is, that they were not making enough money because there were too many of them. *Mail and Empire,* 7 Feb. 1895, 6.

32. The managing director decided how much money was spent in the editorial area of the newspaper. Christopher Bunting was probably responsible for allowing Kit to travel. In her own obituary for him, she wrote that he was kind, "liberal" and her friend when she most needed one. Ibid., 18 Jan. 1896, 5. W.J. Douglas likely took real financial control right after the merger of the *Mail* and the *Empire* and took the title of managing director after Bunting died. Rutherford, *A Victorian Authority,* pp. 107, 239.

33. J.V. MacAree, "When Kit Conducted the Woman's Kingdom," *Mail and Empire,* 14 April 1932, 8. Clipping in PAC K.B.C. Papers, Vol. 2, File 32.

34. PAC K.B.C. Papers, 1987-148 #10. Dated 22 Apr. 1894.

35. Kit variously spelled her daughter's name with and without the "e". The names were her nick-names for them: "Kit Coleman" thanked her "dear friend" Kate Simpson Hayes for her hospitality to her and "Thady" on a trip they took. Saskatchewan Archives Board, Katherine Simpson Hayes Papers, Microfilm #2.15, undated letters file. She referred to "Patsy" helping her at home in a letter to Florence Sherk. PAC Media Club of Canada. Vol. 1. 1913-1920 Triennial Report, 27.

36. *Mail and Empire,* 26 Nov. 1896, Part 3, 4.

37. Ibid., 1 May 1897, Part 3, 4.

38. Ibid., 2 May 1896, 6.

39. Ibid., 15 Aug. 1896, 24.

40. Ibid., 17 Oct. 1896. Part 3, 4 and response to "Merry Sunshine," Ibid., 5 Dec. 1896, Part 3, 5. She later told "An Old Girl" that she and Thady were "like brothers." Ibid., 20 Nov. 1897, Part 2, 4.

41. Ibid., 2 Jan. 1897, Part 3, 4.

42. Ibid., 16 Jan. 1897, Part 3, 4. Thady went away to Trinity College School in Port Hope while Patsy later attended the Quaker College at Pickering, which Kit considered an excellent, and moral, place for her daughter to be. Response to "Wexford," Ibid., 15 July 1899, Part 2, 5; Ibid., 14 Oct. 1899, 17; responses to "Merry Sunshine," Ibid., 5 Dec. 1896, Part 3, 5; confirmed Gartshore-Waterous Interview. In Kathleen Coleman's private papers, there are two similar pieces about a mother leaving her son at school. One is marked "dear old Thad" in her handwriting. PAC K.B.C. Papers, Vol. 2, File 29.

43. *Mail and Empire,* 27 Feb. 1897, Part 3, 4. "Patsey" had been very ill and frail when she was about one year old, a few months after Kit

joined the *Mail*. Response to "All R. Grando," Ibid., 19 Feb. 1898, Part 2, 4.

44. Response to "Enid," Ibid., 5 Mar. 1898, Part 2, 4.
45. Ibid., 25 Dec. 1897, Part 2, 5.
46. Ibid., 5 Mar. 1898, Part 2, 4.
47. Response to "Mater," Ibid., 27 Feb. 1897, Part 3, 4.
48. Ibid., 25 Dec. 1897, Part 2, 5.
49. Response to "Adele," Ibid., 12 Mar. 1898, Part 2, 4.
50. Ibid., 15 Jan.- 22 Feb. 1896, 5. He resurfaced many years later in "The Pedlar's Pack," the column she wrote for *Canada Monthly* magazine from 1911 to 1915. See *Canada Monthly*, Feb. 1911, pp. 303-308.
51. *Mail and Empire*, 27 June 1896, pp. 24, 25.
52. Ibid., 21 Mar. 1896, 5.
53. Ibid., 6 Mar. 1896, 3; Ibid., 11 Mar. 1896, 3.
54. See also "Woman's Kingdom," Ibid., 14 Mar. 1896, 5 and "For and About Women," Ibid., 10 Mar. 1896, 3, which included advice on how a wife should dress for breakfast with her husband. The daily column had disappeared by May 1896 with no explanation.
55. Ibid., 6 Feb. 1897, Part 3, 4; response to "Anxious," Ibid., 13 Feb. 1897, Part 3, 5; Ibid., 20 Feb. 1897, Part 3, 4.
56. Response to "Joey B." On the same page, she reviewed "Keynotes" by George Egerton, a woman author. Ibid., 1 Aug. 1896, 24.
57. Response to "Clericus," Ibid., 14 Dec. 1895, 5.
58. Editorial in the *Mail and Empire*, 28 Dec. 1895, 8. See also "Woman's Kingdom" the same day. Ibid., 5.
59. Ibid., 18 Jan. 1896, 5. See also Robert Craig Brown and Ramsay Cook, *Canada 1896-1921 — A Nation Transformed* (Toronto: McClelland and Stewart 1974), pp. 12-17.
60. *Mail and Empire*, 28 Jan. 1896, 5.
61. "Unrest," Ibid., 1 Feb. 1896, 5.
62. Response to "King," Ibid., 11 July 1896, 24.
63. "Kit's Jubilee Kingdom," Ibid., 10 July 1897, pp. 4, 5, 7.
64. PAC K.B.C Papers, Vol. 1, File 4. Letter from Laurier to Kathleen Blake Watkins dated 19 June, 1897.
65. "Kit In London," *Mail and Empire*, 24 July 1897, Part 2, 1. Other items from her trip and her Correspondence column were carried on page 4.
66. Ibid., 11 Sept. 1897, Part 2, 1.
67. The British newspaper paid three half-pence per line (about one and a half cents). Response to "Anxious," Ibid., 17 July 1909, 17. Kathleen had been invited to lunch with Alfred Harmsworth, the owner of the *Daily Mail* and used the connection to pressure him to get her articles published. Dinner invitation dated Sat. 10 July 1897, and envelope addressed to her at the Covent Garden Hotel,

Victoria St., London, W.C. PAC K.B.C. Papers, Vol. 1, File 6. Letter from Harmsworth dated 7 Aug. 1897, telling her that an article of hers would be published presently. Ibid, File 3.

68. Ibid., file 4, letter from Laurier to Streathfield dated 17 Aug. 1897. Her papers also contain invitations to socials in honour of prominent people, including one from the Duchess of Abercarn for 28 June 1897 to meet the "Indian and Colonial" visitors and on 12 July 1897, an invitation to Sidcup Place in Kent to meet the Premier of Western Australia. There are also a program and a menu with Kathleen's notes about the gathering scribbled on the back. Ibid., File 6.

69. Ibid., File 4, letters from Laurier to Kathleen Blake Watkins dated 23 Dec. 1897 and 8 Feb. 1898.

70. Kit, *To London for the Jubilee*, (Toronto: Morang 1897).

71. Response to "Blue-bell," *Mail and Empire*, 4 Dec. 1897, Part 2, 5.

72. Ibid., 18 Dec. 1897, Part 2, 4.

73. Ibid., 28 May 1898, Part 2, 2.

74. Kit believed it was because her audience had already read most of it in the "Kingdom." Response to "John Bull," Ibid., 22 Oct. 1898, Part 2, 8.

75. There are several clippings, some from American publications, about Kit and the book in Kathleen's scrapbook. PAC K.B.C. Papers, Vol. 3, File 1. Her coverage of the Irish tour was praised in the *Catholic Register* in an article reprinted in the *Mail and Empire*, 20 May 1898, 6.

76. Response to "Tempted," *Daily Mail*, 6 Aug. 1892, 8.

77. *Mail and Empire*, 5 June 1897, Part 3, 4. op. cit.

78. *Daily Mail*, 29 Oct. 1892, 8.

79. Response to "Helped," Ibid., 13 Apr. 1895, 6. Her depression lasted several months. Responses to "Avalon" and "Homesick," *Daily Mail*, 24 Dec. 1892, 8; response to "Under A Cloud," 31 Dec. 1892, 8.

80. *Mail and Empire*, 13 Apr. 1895, 5.

81. *Daily Mail*, 29 June 1894, 5.

82. Response to "Ring Mahone," Ibid., 8 Sept. 1894, 6.

83. Response to "Nameless," Ibid., 1 Feb. 1896, 6. It was not an unusual complaint from a woman journalist. Two of her contemporaries, Ethelwyn Wetherald and Florence Randal (Livesay), mentioned the same problem. Queen's University Archives, W.W. Campbell Papers, 2001b, Box 9, File 003, Ethelwyn Wetherald to W. W. Campbell, 10 Feb 1896; Provincial Archives of Manitoba, Florence Randal Livesay Papers, P 59, Folder 3, Diary entry for 15 Sept. 1904. Further sources on Randal and Wetherald include, respectively, Sandra Gwyn, *The Private Capital* (Toronto: McClelland and Stewart

1984), pp. 317-389 and Margaret Coulby Whitridge, "The Distaff Side of the Confederation Group," in *Atlantis*, Vol. 4, No. 1. Fall 1978.

84. *Mail and Empire*, 19 Oct. 1895, 5.
85. For example, an essay on why men don't marry. Ibid., 23 Oct. 1897, Part 2, 4 (from the *Daily Mail*, 15 July 1893, 5); response to "Harriet" on the intensity of a man's love compared to a woman's. *Mail and Empire*, 9 Oct. 1897, Part 2, 5 (*Daily Mail*, 8 Nov. 1890, 5); response to "Lola" about lesbian love, *Mail and Empire*, 30 Oct. 1897, Part 2, 4 ("Kit's Child," *Daily Mail*, 14 Oct. 1893, 8.) Some years later, a reader caught her plagiarizing an article about ospreys from *Field and Stream*, for which the journalist apologized, explaining that she needed it "to lift me over the stile, for I was a very lame dog that week." *Mail and Empire*, 1 Sept. 1900, 16. The offending article appeared Ibid., 18 August 1900, 16.
86. Response to "Constance," *Daily Mail*, 6 Aug. 1892, 8.
87. "Three Phantoms," Ibid., 5. She later wrote that the unsigned poems that had appeared in the "Kingdom" over the years were her own. *Mail and Empire*, 4 May 1895, 5.
88. Response to "Hilda," *Daily Mail*, 28 Jan. 1893, 8 and "Ken," Ibid., 29 Apr. 1893, 8.
89. *Mail and Empire*, 3 Oct. 1896, Part 3, 4; Ibid., 27 May 1899, 16.
90. Response to "Fanny," *Daily Mail*, 9 Dec. 1893, 5.
91. Ibid., 4 Feb. 1893, 8.
92. Ibid., 10 Nov. 1894, 6. Her comments appeared in response to a question about lesbianism. Kit was reassuring a correspondent that strong emotional ties between girls or women were normal, but that sexual expression of those feelings would lead to mental illness. The question came up in the first place because the journalist's admonishments to "Kit's Child" about her "insane love for another girl" had confused one of her readers. Ibid., 22 July 1893, 8; see also Ibid., 14 Oct. 1893, 8; *Mail and Empire*, 18 May 1895, 6; Ibid., 29 Feb. 1896, 6. At the time, the emotional, even sensual, closeness that had been considered a normal element of friendships between women was coming under the scrutiny of sexologists such as Havelock Ellis. See Carroll Smith-Rosenberg, "The Female World of Love and Ritual: Relations Between Women in Nineteenth-Century America" in *Signs*, Vol. 1 (Autumn 1975), repr. in *Disorderly Conduct;* also Lillian Faderman, *Surpassing the Love of Men: Romantic Friendship and Love Between Women from the Renaissance to the Present* (New York: William Morrow and Company 1981), Introduction. See also Kit's disgusted responses to a genuinely disturbed "Janet" of Peterborough, who persistently wrote her love letters. They include *Mail and Empire* 21 June, 1905, 18; Ibid., 5 Aug. 1905, 18; Ibid., 9 June 1906, 21; Ibid., 13 Apr. 1907, 18.

93. Response to "Valerie Bergmann," *Daily Mail*, 29 Dec. 1894, 5.
94. Blewett was women's page editor of the *Globe* twice; the second time, as "Katharine Kent," from 1917-1925. See her obituary in the *Globe and Mail*, 20 August, 1934, 1; also Ibid., 21 August 1934, 8. For an anthology of her poems, see Jean Blewett, *Jean Blewett's Poems* (Toronto: McClelland and Stewart 1922).
95. *Mail and Empire*, 21 Oct. 1893, 5; response to "Nina R.," *Mail and Empire*, 16 Nov. 1895, 6; response to "Mayflower," Ibid., 28 Dec. 1895, 5.
96. Ibid., 22 Feb. 1896, 6. A poem entitled "All" and signed "Kathleen Blake Watkins" appeared two weeks later. It was the first time Kit had signed her real name to anything on her "Woman's Kingdom" page. It appeared below a poem written by Jean Blewett, entitled "Past." They were similar in style and were about lost love. Ibid., 7 Mar. 1896, 6.
97. Response to "Kitty Gray," Ibid., 13 Nov. 1897, Part 2, 4.

CHAPTER 4
THE WAR CORRESPONDENT

In 1898, North American newspapers were full of articles that denigrated Spain as weak, corrupt and unable to prevent its oppressed Cuban subjects from allying with their strong, young neighbour, the United States of America.[1] Several North American newspapers gleefully took bets on the outcome of the tensions between Spain and the U.S.[2] Kit saw that the Americans had an economic stake in winning Cuba, with its sugar and tobacco crops, and was upset by what she saw as war-mongering by politicians and "...those newspaper wreckers! With their screetching [sic] headlines and their $50,000 bets!"[3] She was not impressed by their appeals to nobility of spirit in potential American volunteer soldiers:

> As to the humane aspects of the case—"To the rescue of Cuba!" Certainly: but O my Masters!... What of America's treatment of the Red Man? The irony of these things is exquisite.[4]

Kit had grown up amid fierce sectarian fighting in Ireland and had never liked war. Whenever one broke out, she always criticized newspapers for their jingoism.[5] The Cuban conflict was no different:

> We lose sight of the sadness of war when we are confronted with the big headlines in the newspapers that exploit bombardments and battles, and the blowing up of ships, and the victory of the one side over the other. We do not see the limbs

> of men torn asunder, nor hear the choking cries of the
> wounded as they drift down with the sinking ships. We do
> not think of the shocking desolation that will sweep over the
> hearts of the mothers and the wives and the sisters of the poor
> fellows who go under. All this is hidden from us. We see only
> the headlines. We think only of the Stock Exchange. When
> there are no battles, it is not good business for the news-
> mongers. When there are, the more blood and bones that can
> be put into the announcements, the finer the "sensation"...It
> is on woman that war falls heaviest.[6]

Her sentiments would not necessarily have alienated her readers. There were many Canadians who, influenced by the liberal reform movements of the time, preferred to believe that rational negotiation could prevent armed conflicts.[7] But, at the same time, the newspapers gloried in war stories. British and American war correspondents, who covered the first American attack on Cuba from a press despatch boat near the battle scene,[8] had heroic stature, especially in their own eyes. One journalist described them as:

> ...men of daring, resource and ability, who are attracted by
> the fascination of war, and by a desire to play a part, however
> humble, in the most awful, grim, and tragic drama enacted
> on the human stage. They are handsomely paid for their ser-
> vices. There is no restriction on them in the matter of expense,
> for the newspapers are only too ready and willing to spend
> enormous sums of money for fresh and important news from
> the seat of war. The chief qualifications for this hard and
> adventurous life are physical strength, the endurance to sub-
> sist for days on a meager supply of inferior food, and to sleep
> at night in the open; iron nerves and mental vigour; sound
> sense and rapid judgement; a quick, observant eye, capable
> of taking in the ever-shifting scenes and changing incidents
> of a field of battle, and a ready, vivid pen to convey one's
> impressions on paper. The war correspondent is often, in the
> discharge of his duty, to run as great a risk of being killed
> or wounded as any soldier in the fighting line. It has fallen
> to him often, also, to render a great service to the Army which
> he accompanies in the field....[9]

As a journalist, the adventure-seeking Kit was excited by the Cuban conflict, despite her antipathy towards war. "I wish I were a man. I would be somewhere in it."[10] Although

106

she knew that "they wouldn't let a lace flounce over the side
of a cruiser for all the money in the United States treasury,"[11]
by early May 1898, she was in Washington, acquiring press
accreditation from the U.S. Army.[12] She had somehow persuaded the *Mail and Empire* to send her to war.

how ?

At first, she reported, the U.S. Secretary of War, General
R.A. Alger, did not want her to travel with the army soldiers, who would be pitching tents in rough settings under
a hot sun and "'lounging around half-dressed. It is no place
at all for a lady.'"[13] But he relented after she used her professional and social connections,[14] particularly her friendship with the president of the International Press Union of
Women Journalists, Mary Lockwood,[15] and her acquaint-
anceship with Lady Aberdeen, officials of the Canadian
branch of the Red Cross Society and the British Ambassador
to Washington, Sir Julian Pauncefote. Noted the *Boston
Transcript*:

> Being a lady by birth and in the best sense of the word, she
> has been fortunate in preserving as friends people with posi-
> tion with whom newspaper work has brought her in contact,
> owing to the tact and discrimination she has shown in never
> overstepping the bounds between what is legitimate for the
> public to know and what good taste prompts to withhold
> from publication.[16]

The *Mail and Empire's* decision to send a woman to war
should not be seen as a new commitment to equality of the
sexes in journalism, but as a "stunt" obviously designed to
boost circulation. A front-page announcement assured readers that Kit would send back reports "which will certainly
prove to Canadians, at least, the most vividly interesting of
any that will be penned from the scene of conflict."[17] Her
newspaper also ran prominent subscription advertisements:
"'Kit' as a War Correspondent. The Only Lady Ever
Accredited to this Position now represents the Mail and
Empire at the Seat of War."[18] In fact, at least two other
women journalists were accredited to cover the war in Cuba,
although they received their papers after Kit did. They were
a Miss Curtis Wager-Smith of the *Philadelphia Inquirer*[19] and

Clara B. Colby of the Washington *Woman's Tribune.*[20] Two other women—Anna Benjamin of *Leslie's Illustrated Weekly* and Mrs. Trumbull White, of the Chicago *Record*, who was also acting as a Red Cross nurse—were in Cuba at the same time Kit was, but it is not clear if they were actually accredited as war correspondents.[21]

Rival newspapers saw Kit's assignment as an attempt to add to the *Mail and Empire's* circulation. Nevertheless, the *Catholic Register* expected her, as a woman, to provide maternal insights on the horrors of war and the hospital services provided for young soldiers at the front. In fact, her gender was seen as an advantage:

> That her letters from the war-field will be graphic and brilliant there is no doubt, and perhaps there is no woman writer today who could better pourtray [sic] the awful horrors of modern war, and bring home to the mothers and daughters of English-speaking people the brutality and barbarity of war, unless as a last resource... being a woman among the nurses she will be in a position to gain information of intense interest about the hospital service such as no male war correspondent has ever yet been able to gather on the field at first hand.[22]

Her female colleagues were intrigued with her new assignment. "Polly" of the Chicago *Times-Herald* envied her, praised her journalistic abilities and commented with an insight that suggested she knew the temperamental Kit well:

> A strange, pathetic, fiery, alluring, talented personality has gone to Tampa, and I watch the outcome curiously. The woman war correspondent is a new quantity. We shall prove her mettle to the world. It is a rare chance that has come to Kit and if I know her at all, she is tossing about the prize in her little hand, viewing it disdainfully and saying, "What's the use?" and at the same time is doing her level best to out-write every male correspondent on the field.[23]

"M.H.L." of *The Register* respected Kit for her decision to go to Cuba, even though she was leaving behind—perhaps forever—her two children. Both son Thady, then aged about 13, and daughter Patsy, then about 11, were already well known to her newspaper readers since their mother wrote of them often. For "M.H.L," her leaving them was not grounds for criticism, but for professional praise:

> Poor Kit! away off amidst horrors of which you are only now on the outskirts, the greatest pledge you could have given of the earnestness of your work was, that you were willing to leave your children, your Patsy and Thady, whom you so strongly love; when such love gives place to duty, duty will surely be well performed.[24]

The journalist made it clear to her readers that she had volunteered for the job and was not only determined to survive the experience but make a success of it:

> I am going of my own free will and desire...I have no doubt but like the cat and the proverbial bad penny, I shall eventually come back. Regarding the work in hand to do, the lexicon of youth is not the only dictionary that has the word "fail" expurgated from its pages. The thought of two little children somewhere in Canada, and the thought of the dear north land, with her summers and her snows, will often crowd in upon and efface every other....[25]

The *Mail and Empire* treated her appointment as a novelty, at the same time, making it clear that her work would not "conflict" with that of male correspondents. She was to "supplement" their breaking news coverage, which was supplied to the newspaper in a cooperative arrangement with the London *Times* and the *New York Herald*.[26] Later, as she and the other correspondents waited in Tampa, Florida, for the order to move on Cuba, she explained to her readers:

> There is very little news going, but I am not here to detail the serious events of the war (which have not yet commenced) rather am I here to write that light and airy matter which is ignominiously termed, by the trade, guff, but which is not always easy to manufacture.[27]

It could be argued that her secondary reporting role gave her a lot more flexibility in what she could write about, especially since she was not under the same deadline pressure as the male correspondents. In fact, she tried to pass on any "scoops" that may have interested them. But her attempts at collegiality did not help her win their favour. Both the newspapermen and the American authorities prevented her from getting to Cuba in time to cover the major battles. In the end, she arrived as the war ended and wrote vivid descriptions of the destruction and suffering it had brought about—a record that did not get front-page coverage but provided a more encompassing view than daily reports of skirmishes.[28]

At Tampa, as war correspondents and soldiers waited to be transported to Cuba, British newspapermen took Kit under their wing. But even so, being a woman was difficult. The male journalists, who kept busy buying horses, tents and other supplies, teased her about the kind of dress and gear she would acquire. Their jesting may have raised doubts in her own mind about her role, but she kept her tone light:

> The boys suggest a bronco, Mexican saddle, short hair, and— bloomers, but I am dickering for a ride behind each one of them, day about, in return for which I guarantee to sew on buttons and do the cooking... There are many things a woman can and may do, but the line may be very safely drawn at army correspondent. However, nous verrons, as they say in France.[29]

Her feminine flippancy did not fool her male colleagues. Charles E. Hands of the London *Daily Mail* described her as "a tall, healthy, youngish woman, with a quiet, self-reliant manner and an alert, intelligent, enterprising look."[30] At first, he wrote, the men regarded her presence among them as "comic" and her desire to get to Cuba "absurd." But she was determined to get there, she told the skeptical Hands, "and not all the old generals in the old army are going to stop me."[31]

Kit told him that she was not going there to write big war stories "'in the grand style such as you boys write, but just the poor woman's side of the war, don't you see?'"[32]

In fact, Hands wrote, she earned the respect of the other journalists by her industry. She was awake and out looking

"MRS. BLAKE WATKINS"

And How She Proved Herself One of "the Boys" at Tampa.

LADY WAR CORRESPONDENT

She Was Alone Among the Men— They Pitied Her, but She Asked No Favors, and Found Plenty of "Beats."

From The London Mail.

It was a day of hopeless desolation. Everything was all wrong. The Spanish fleet, for which we had been waiting for a fortnight,

Charles E. Hands' account of Kit the war correspondent as it appeared in the *New York Times* 1898.

for scoops long before the other journalists. She sometimes succeeded, being fluent in Spanish as well as French and English. "Every time we meet her, she tells us of some interesting little incident she heard of, or discovered or invented," he wrote. Most of the stories she shared with the men were colourful anecdotes, but, according to Hands, she informed them that the U.S. Army planned to land a cargo of ammunition and food for the insurgents in Cuba, information her male colleagues had been unsuccessful at pinning down.[33]

There were several such plans and it is not clear which one Hands meant. Brown believes it was the ill-fated attempt to smuggle a shipment of arms and ammunition in the archaic side-wheel steamer "Gussie" in early May 1898,[34] an embarrassing episode that was given front-page coverage in the *Mail and Empire*.[35] According to the datelines on her articles—which should not be taken as accurate—Kit did not arrive in Tampa until almost two weeks later.[36]

Certainly her byline does not appear on any such story, perhaps because it was understood that the "hard news" was to be relayed by the male members of the London *Times—New York Herald—Mail and Empire* team.

Hands' article notwithstanding,[37] it is clear from her own writing that Kit was not treated as an equal by the male newspaper correspondents. A few weeks after she arrived in Tampa, she wrote of dining and sitting alone, with only the hotel's tropical birds and pet monkey for company, while army officers and the male journalists, who were royally treated by the hotel staff, entertained themselves nearby. To the news that twelve of the newspapermen were self-importantly setting up their own correspondents' "mess" in an "Army of Invasion" tent—the better to prepare themselves for Cuba—Kit commented:

> I believe I will set up my own solitary camp and call it "Woman War Correspondent's Mess, Army of Opposition, Scoops For Sale Here." The woman war correspondent has been called the unknown quantity. She is carefully ostracized. She is not young and pretty. Generals will have nothing to

112

do with her. She shall be left behind. The great army of press-
men shall move forward jeering at her. She shall not produce
"copy."[38]

The copy she did produce in Tampa was on topics ranging from the best battle strategy likely to be employed by
the United States—in which she described the Spanish as
filthy and the Americans as heroes[39]—to more maternal
concerns about the young, green, American soldiers. In one
sentimental vignette, she was being given a tour of a U.S.
army camp when she heard the strains of "Home Sweet
Home" coming from a tent. Upon lifting the flap, she saw
a young American volunteer, playing the soulful tune on
his harmonica. Instantly reminded of her own son, she
wrote:

> I cannot express to you the feeling that came over me...I sup-
> pose it is because one is a woman, and a bit emotional, that
> the tears come to one's eyes; but I dropped the flap without
> a word, and there was something besides the sun in my eyes
> as we walked silently on. One is beginning to realize what
> war means, and I tell you it is poor and squalid, and a bit
> heartbreaking...[40]

By June 23, most of the war correspondents had joined
military units or had otherwise made their way to Cuba.[41]
But despite the fact that she had authorization from the
Secretary of War, General R.A. Alger, to go with the troops,
"if not inconsistent with the best interests of the service,"[42]
Kit was left behind. As she had predicted, none of the military leaders would give her passage. She complained to her
readers:

> For be it known unto you that the gods who preside over the
> destinies of Women and War have decided that these two
> shall not meet. "Cupid is the god for women", thunders Jove,
> "Mars for men." And great generals brushed me away as
> though I were an impertinent fly.[43]

There may have been another reason. Years later, she
claimed that she was briefly arrested by what she referred
to as the American "secret service" for ignoring military censorship rules and sending a coded message to her editor that

the troops were about to leave Florida for Cuba. Her editor, she wrote, was furious with her for getting caught.[44] It is difficult to know if her story was true. There appears to be no official verification of it, perhaps because the military authorities were quite careful not to record the details of the secret service's activities, even on the invoices for expenses incurred by its operations.[45]

The unknown writer of an article which appeared in *Town Topics* and was reprinted in the *Mail and Empire* indignantly made it clear that not only was the army reluctant to take Kit, the most telling opposition to her presence came from many of the male war correspondents. Despite the influence of the military authorities in Washington, the newspapermen won the day:

> The army would not be responsible for her, the one hundred and fifty or more newspapermen would not have their glory dimmed by a woman doing the same work they were doing—she in tame feminine apparel, and they in sombreros, duck, knives, belts, cartridges and revolvers....They were not in mental condition to recognize the genuine, honest, determined worker, who could work with the same understanding, courage and keen observation as they themselves.[46]

Kit also laid most of the blame for her inability to get to Cuba on the male war correspondents. Some months later, when the rival Toronto *Globe* boasted of its own success in getting news out of Cuba, she wrote indignantly:

> This unlucky person quite failed—owing to her sex—to go "with the troops from Tampa." She was very keenly made to feel her inferiority by some of the gallant male members of the press, who, she was informed on what she supposes to be fair authority, did all in their power to prevent her from attaining the object of her mission, as well as otherwise depressing and harassing her.

Newspapermen from the west, it appears, took her part and "did all they could to cheer and help,"[47] but were outnumbered by many from the eastern papers.[48]

Kit sent off a frantic telegram to her journalist friend in Washington, Mary Lockwood, asking her to get General Alger to arrange passage for her on a Red Cross boat that had been put under naval jurisdiction. "No time to loose [sic]. Every other avenue closed," Kit's message read.[49] Permission was granted[50] and on July 15, the *Mail and Empire* made her departure for Santiago front page news.[51] But it turned out to be a false alarm. Again, Kit had been left behind.

According to the writer of the *Town Topics* article, the Red Cross head nurse in charge of the organization's medical services in Cuba during the war, Clara Barton, refused to give Kit passage on the Red Cross boat,[52] despite the telegram from the office of the Secretary of War and a subsequent telegram from General Alger himself, which he sent at Kit's request.[53] It is not clear why she was turned down, but she never seemed to bear any ill-will toward Barton, whose efforts to help the wounded and sick she later praised in an effusive article.[54] Several years later, in other versions of her adventures, Kit explained that Barton did, at one point, allow her on board a Red Cross steam yacht with two Cuban women and a number of officials. The boat, which was under the command of Barton's nephew, tried to make the 600-mile journey to Santiago but was turned back by high seas and arrived at the "mined" harbour in Key West, crippled.[55]

After her failure to get passage from Tampa, Kit had made her way to Key West, hoping to get to Cuba from there. At that point, she was deeply discouraged and tempted to return home. But her professional pride—and the reputation of the *Mail and Empire*—were at stake. She noted that people she met praised her newspaper for trying to send a woman correspondent to Cuba, as hopeless as the venture was turning out to be, and she was still expected to produce copy wherever she was. Her instructions from her editor had been "'send a word when you can, and how you can', which is all that one can do," so she persevered.[56]

About three weeks after Kit arrived in Key West, a telegram from "K.B. Watkins" and a Doctor C.R. Gill was sent to Mary Lockwood in Washington, telling her that some Red Cross doctors and nurses had been stranded in Key West and needed passage to Cuba immediately, preferably on a naval supply boat, the "Niagara."[57]

On July 22, the captain of that same boat recorded in his log that, on orders from the Secretary of the Navy, he picked up several passengers at Key West including "Mrs. Blake Watkins" for passage to Santiago.[58]

Two weeks later, in a prominent, front page article datelined July 28, Kit announced to her readers: "After nearly three months despairing efforts to get here, the great force which we call will has conquered. I am looking at the hills of Cuba."[59] But another headline of the same page made it clear she was too late to see action: "No Doubt Now the War is Over," it read.[60]

Undaunted, she travelled to the scenes of battles to record their aftermath. She slept in the open in the hills outside of Santiago "in a boy's rubber suit" to avoid being raped or murdered and rode her horse astride as she travelled from one grim battleground to another, a story she told only later.[61] She sent back vivid descriptions of the destruction she saw and did not spare her sympathy for the defeated Spanish soldiers, many of whom died in the most gruesome circumstances.

Once, travelling by boat, she reached the scene of the great naval battle of the war, about forty-eight miles outside of Santiago de Cuba, where the Spanish fleet had been defeated by the U.S. Navy. She reported that the despairing captain of one ship, the "Almirante Oquendo," had gotten his crew drunk, locked them below, set fire to the cruiser and then committed suicide. In fact, her report was quite wrong. The "Almirante Oquendo's" captain, Joaquin Maria Lazaga, actually died of a heart attack shortly after surrendering his ship, which had been hit by American fire fifty-seven times.[62]

When Kit got to the scene she found the bodies of Spanish sailors scattered all over the beach along with the battered remains of their ships. Judging from a photograph taken at the time, her description of the "Almirante Oquendo" was accurate, at least, if somewhat dramatic:

> ...(it) lay, half upon the beach, like some dying monster that had tried to crawl up out of the sea and had died in the attempt... Half burnt rope ends dangled in the masts. Torn edges of iron flared out everywhere. You would think an army of demons had been let loose from hell to twist, and smash, and batter the ships, to torture and burn and wreak impish cruelties on the men and beasts. What these Spanish sailors must have suffered on that July day in the blinding smoke and heat and stress of this terrible battle cannot be told by human lips or written by any pen.[63]

Her report that Captain Lazaga had committed suicide might have been a war rumour, rather than a fantasy of her own invention. She later maintained that it was male war correspondents who often fabricated stories from Cuba, and she never did or would:

> I think the woman reporter is more honest or reliable under certain conditions than her brother craftsmen, or, it may be that she is only more timid. In any case, no press woman could endure to sully her work by false dispatches. This much I will say for the very often misjudged and underpaid newspaper woman.[64]

Besides her vivid descriptions of the scenes of battle, Kit also wrote of the suffering endured by the beaten and fever-ravaged Spanish soldiers she saw in Santiago before she left for home:

> A dreadful, dreadful sight. Men were there whose hairs had fallen off their heads, across which the skin was so tightly stretched that it revealed the formation of every skull distinctly. Eyes sunken deep in their sockets burnt like dim lamps on the edge of extinction. Yellow as a guinea was the colour of men's faces...The men were past despair, past feeling. And yet life lingered. Death crept forward by inches. Pitiful, weak, moaning, there they lay, praying for release from the misery of living. It is awful. It changes one's whole

view of things. It sobers and saddens, inexpressibly saddens one.[65]

The badly trained and wounded American soldiers were also stricken with fever. Their own government had not provided them with a hospital ship or enough food or medical supplies, a fact that was driven painfully home to Kit when she accompanied scores of them back to Tampa on board the "Comal," a transport vessel. There was not enough food, water, or medicine. She and the other newspaper correspondents donated their quinine and other medical supplies and she helped the only doctor on board nurse the soldiers. In an article describing these conditions, Kit alluded to mismanagement of both the war and the evacuation of the American troops but refused to lay specific blame on anyone, saying it was better to wait until all the facts were known.[66] She wrote about the nightmare on board more fully only years later:

> Sixteen days in a loathsome transport, with one hundred and thirty-three men in every stage of sickness, living on rotten rations and apparently forgotten by the country for which they were suffering....One becomes a machine. There is nothing for pity, or sympathy or hope to feed upon. There is little even for despair. It is the last to go, and then only the body lives, the bones move, the dull brain answers only to the call of duty, the dull ears heed not the outcries of the sick, the dull eyes see not the ghastliness of gaping wounds. It is all the same! What matter if the feet slip in blood instead of rain?[67]

She admitted that she never wrote the "miserable story of Cuba" because the U.S. Secretary of War, General R.A. Alger "begged me to refrain..."[68]

At Tampa, she and the other passengers were kept waiting on board the "Comal" for days before being allowed to board the U.S. flagship "Seguranca," where food and medicine were in better supply.[69] Still, upon her arrival in New York, the sight of a full glass of milk waiting for her in her hotel room, after she had witnessed and experienced weeks of deprivation, produced "a hurricane of tears, the breakdown after all those hideous days and nights..."[70] There were times, she told her readers, when she wondered if she would survive the Cuba ordeal and see her children again:

> The last letters to the chicks—the poor chicks! and to the few other dear ones—such a little circle! were written and laid aside to be given "in the event of my death in Cuba." And yet back I toddled, hale and well, without a scratch or fever. God be thanked! Only a bit shocked and full of tears... Then the chicks! Thade was up to my eyebrows when I left and he's a bang length over my crown, now, and Pattikins is creeping up from her nook under my arm. It was great to be half-strangled by them when they saw me.[71]

She told her readers she never wanted to be a war correspondent again,[72] although time and distance from the event changed her mind.[73]

A few readers criticized Kit for going to Cuba in the first place,[74] but she received a great deal of professional recognition and praise for her work. Her colleague, "The Flaneur," quoted the editor of an influential U.S. daily, who pronounced it "....the best work I have seen since the war broke out." The unnamed editor went on to describe her literary style as "...the work of an artist...infused with a certain, subtle, human sympathy..."[75]

Her sister-journalists were certainly impressed. She was invited to speak before the International Press Union of Women Journalists in Washington, an occasion which the privately-shy Kit claimed she found more nerve-wracking than Cuba itself:

> And you read your little paper in fear and trembling before a solemn audience of special correspondents and editors of women's pages, and wish you were any place on earth—even in Santiago—rather than standing there under that stream of light, reading something you didn't understand, in a strange voice you had never heard before. You had to steady yourself against the table or you would have fallen flat down, and your hands shivered so that the leaves of your paper began a tremolo symphony of their own that was fearsome.[76]

119

For awhile, Kit became a public heroine[77] with imitators—women claiming that they had also gone off to the Spanish-American War. She wrote that she was, as far as she knew, the only woman to be issued a war press pass by the United States government[78] and the only female war correspondent in Cuba.[79] She never mentioned seeing any of the other women who were there.

Her adventures may have made her famous, but they did not improve her finances. Some years later, she complained in a private letter to a *Mail and Empire* colleague, Katherine Hale, that when she had returned from Cuba "absolutely coinless," she was rebuffed by the *Mail and Empire*'s tight-fisted business manager, whom she described as "the mean-est soul that ever was put into a body."[80] In addition, she could not persuade the newspaper to help her publish a book of her Cuba columns or any other descriptions of her adventures, similar to her earlier one about Queen Victoria's Diamond Jubilee.[81] As she explained to one reader, Cuba was already "old news":

> So you were disappointed that you did not hear more of my Cuban experiences "since the *Mail* advertised it so." Well, you would have had a good deal more, only it was repre-sented that the public had gotten tired of war stories and wanted no more of the Yanko-Spanko experiences.[82]

Kit's work in Cuba was recognized in the end mainly because of her own determination to overcome almost insurmountable opposition. While she was there, she used her professional skills to send back home the best and most colourful work she could. Like her male colleagues, she paid some lip service to American military interests by not reveal-ing the extent of their mismanagement of the war. In other words, she tried to keep on the good side of the authorities. But in her own way, particularly with her descriptions of the damage the war caused, she condemned it. She was most able to do this by allowing herself to be "female," that is, by letting her maternalism take over and express concern, for example, for the ill-prepared, fever-stricken and dying soldiers on all sides of the conflict.

Her adventure cost her. She was physically weaker—she had contracted malaria[83]—as well as emotionally shaken. The Cuba experience, she later wrote, "broke my health for all time"[84] and seemed to have brought to a head the unhappiness and insecurity that had been plaguing her for years. She tried to solve her dilemma by choosing emotional stability in her private life and abandoning her ambitions. Upon her return from the war, she married Doctor Theobald Coleman, who had been courting her for some time.[85] But it was many years before she found real peace of mind.

Notes

1. See the *Mail and Empire*, 3 Apr. 1898, Part 2, 3.
2. Newspaper coverage of the conflict is examined by Joseph E. Wisan, *The Cuban Crisis as Reflected in the New York Press (1895-1898)* (New York: Octagon Books 1965).
3. *Mail and Empire*, 23 Apr. 1898, Part 2, 4 and response to "Your American Subject," Ibid., 5. Some writers have since claimed the war was virtually started by the *New York Journal* and the *World* in a sensational, jingoistic battle for circulation. For example, Phillip Knightley, *The First Casualty* (New York and London: Harcourt, Brace and Jovanovich 1975), pp. 55-59. But journalism historian Marvin N. Olasky and other academics have argued that those newspapers did not characterize the national mood. Marvin Olasky, "Hawks or Doves: Texas Press and Spanish-American War", *Journalism Quarterly*, Vol. 64, No. 1. Spring 1987, pp. 205-211.
4. *Mail and Empire*, 30 Apr. 1898, Part 2, 4. Historians have long argued over the causes of the war. See Philip S. Foner, *The Spanish-Cuban-American War and the Birth of American Imperialism 1895-1902*, Vols. I & II (New York and London: Monthly Review Press 1972).
5. *Daily Mail*, 10 Sept. 1892, 5. See also her criticism of newspaper reports about the Chinese-Korean conflict. Ibid., 11 Aug. 1894, 5.
6. *Mail and Empire* 7 May 1898, Part 2, 4.
7. Thomas P. Socknat, *Witness Against War: Pacifism in Canada 1900-1945* (Toronto: University of Toronto Press 1987), 41.
8. *Mail and Empire*, 28 Apr. 1898, 1.
9. Michael MacDonagh, "Position of the War Correspondent," Ibid., 30 Apr. 1898, Part 2, 2, reprinted from *Fortnightly*. See also Knightley, pp. 42-55.
10. *Mail and Empire*, 30 Apr. 1898, Part 2, 4 and response to "Tommy A.," Ibid., 5.
11. Ibid., 7 May 1898, Part 2, 4.
12. National Archives of the United States, Records of the Military, RG 107, Records of the Office of the Secretary of War, General Correspondence, File No. 3093, War Correspondent's Pass No. 119, dated 3 May 1898.
13. *Mail and Empire*, 14 May, 1898 Part 2, 4.
14. See letters from W.J. Douglas, the General Manager of the *Mail and Empire*, to the Assistant Secretary of War asking for press accreditation for Kit, and to the Commanders of the *New York Herald* despatch boats, asking them to give her passage "if possible." National Archives, Records of the Military, RG107, Records of the Office of the Secretary of War. General Correspondence 1898, File No. 3093.

15. Her telegram to Lockwood asked if she could join the Red Cross as a nurse, in order to get "to the front as correspondent." She asked Lockwood to use her influence with the President of the Red Cross, Clara Barton. Lockwood passed the telegram on to a Mr. Russell of the Department of Justice who in turn sent it to the Assistant Secretary of State, J.B. Moors. Moors wrote to George D. Meiklejohn, the Assistant Secretary of War, saying Russell had told him that "Mrs. Watkins has been instrumental in keeping the 'Mail' in an attitude favorable to our cause in the pending conflict with Spain." Telegram to Mrs. Mary Lockwood from Kit, dated 25 April, 1898; letter from Moors to Meiklejohn, dated 30 April, 1898. Ibid. See also the Washinton *Woman's Tribune*, 11 Mar. 1899. Clipping in PAC K.B.C. Papers, Vol. 3, File 1.

16. PAC K.B.C. Papers, Vol. 3, File 1, undated clipping from the *Boston Transcript*.

17. *Mail and Empire*, 19 May 1898, 1.

18. Ibid., 21 May 1898, 7.

19. National Archives of the United States, Records of the Military, RG 107, Records of the Office of the Secretary of War, General Correspondence, File No. 4439, dated 8 June 1898.

20. Ibid., No. 4851, dated 21 June 1898.

21. Charles H. Brown, *The Correspondents' War* (New York: Charles Scribner's Sons 1967), pp. 210-213.

22. Reprinted in the *Mail and Empire*, 20 May 1898, 6.

23. Quoted in the *Mail and Empire*, 24 May 1898, 10.

24. Undated clipping from *The Register* in PAC K.B.C. Papers, Vol. 3, File 1, Scrapbook. The children were at boarding schools near Toronto at the time. "'Kit' and Her Work," *Mail and Empire*, 11 June 1898, Part 2, 4, reprinted from the *Reporter*, Galt, Ontario.

25. *Mail and Empire*, 21 May 1898, Part 2, 4.

26. Subscription ad in the *Mail and Empire*. Ibid., 7. Brown writes that Anna Benjamin was not meant to do spot news and compete with the male war correspondents, either. He takes her colour articles seriously but devalues Kit's dispatches to the *"Mail and Express"* [sic] as "sob sister" copy. Brown, "A Woman's Odyssey: the War Correspondence of Anna Benjamin," *Journalism Quarterly*, Autumn 1969, pp. 522-530.

27. *Mail and Empire*, 8 June 1898, 10. But it did mean that, for once, she was able to leave "Woman's Kingdom" in other hands and concentrate on her Cuba assignment. Her editors used syndicated women's features under the title "Of Interest To Women" in her absence. See, for example, Ibid., Part 2, 4.

28. American journalists Rheta Childe Dorr and Bessie Beatty were also assigned secondary roles by their editors when they covered the

Russian Revolution of 1917-1918, with similar journalistic results. McGlashan, op. cit., pp. 54-61.

29. *Mail and Empire*, 26 May 1898, 5.
30. Reprinted as "The London Daily Mail Writes About 'Kit'," in the *Mail and Empire*, 25 June 1898, Part 2, 4; reprinted as "'Mrs. Blake Watkins' and How She Proved Herself One of 'the Boys' at Tampa," in the *New York Times*, 3 July 1898, 13.
31. Ibid. In his article, Brown attributes this quote to Anna Benjamin, rather than Kit. The version in his book is the correct one. Brown, "A Woman's Odyssey, 525; *The Correspondents' War*, 210. The mistake is repeated in Marzolf, pp. 27-28.
32. "The London Daily Mail Writes About 'Kit'," in the *Mail and Empire*, 25 June 1898, Part 2, 4.
33. Ibid.
34. Brown, *The Correspondents' War*, pp. 213-220.
35. *Mail and Empire*, 14 May 1898, 1.
36. Her first article from there was datelined 26 May. Ibid., 28 May 1898, Part 2, 4. A dateline at the head of an article indicates the place and time of writing, but it was not unusual for a journalist to write the article several days after he or she actually witnessed the events described. This was especially true of colour, or feature, stories as opposed to "hard news," which was telegraphed to the newspaper as quickly as possible.
37. The Galt *Reporter* commented, "Some of the American papers have had long accounts of 'Kit', all more or less ridiculous." See "'Kit' and Her Work," op. cit.
38. *Mail and Empire*, 31 May 1898, 2.
39. Ibid., 25 May 1898, 10. Her later description of poverty-stricken Cubans in Key West was also very racist. Ibid., 2 July 1898, Part 2, 4.
40. Ibid., 26 May 1898, 5.
41. Brown, *The Correspondents' War*, 308.
42. A note from R.A. Alger to the Commanding General of the United States Forces, dated 6 June 1898. Copy in PAC K.B.C. Papers, Vol. 1, File 3.
43. *Mail and Empire*, 20 June 1898, 2.
44. In her column, entitled "The Pedlar's Pack," *Canada Monthly*, Oct. 1911, pp. 463-464; Ibid., Nov. 1914, 40.
45. National Archives of the United States, Records of the Military, RG 107, Records of the Office of the Secretary of War, General Correspondence, letter from L.P. Mitchell, Assistant Comptroller to W.S. Yeatman, Disbursing Clerk, War Dept. dated 16 June 1898.
46. *Mail and Empire* 15 July 1898, 1, reprinted from *Town Topics*.
47. *Mail and Empire*, 28 Jan. 1899, Part 2, pp. 4-5.

48. The *Globe's* correspondent, John A. Ewan, was an exception. He had apparently supported her attempts to get to Cuba. Ibid., 20 June 1898, 2. Brown writes that there were several hundred reporters but the U.S. Army would accommodate only 89 of the male journalists. Brown, "A Woman's Odyssey," 525.
49. National Archives of the United States, Records of the Military, RG 107, Records of the Office of the Secretary of War, General Correspondence, File No. 4526, telegram from Kit to Mary Lockwood, dated 14 June 1898.
50. Ibid., letter from the Assistant Secretary of War to Mary Lockwood, quoting a telegram sent to Kit that day, authorizing her to accompany a Red Cross contingent to Cuba. Letter dated 15 June 1898.
51. *Mail and Empire*, 15 July 1898, 1.
52. *Mail and Empire* 15 July 1898, 1, reprinted from *Town Topics*, op. cit.
53. National Archives of the United States, Records of the Military, RG 107, Records of the Office of the Secretary of War, General Correspondence, telegram from Kathleen Blake Watkins to Gen. Alger, dated 23 June 1898; telegram from R.A. Alger to Kathleen Blake Watkins dated 25 June 1898—copy of same in PAC K.B.C. Papers Vol. 1, File 3.
54. *Mail and Empire*, 13 Aug. 1898, Part 2, 4.
55. "Kit's Column," Stratford *Daily Beacon*, 23 Sept. 1911, 11; Ibid., 27 Apr. 1912, 9. Once Kit finally did make it to Santiago, Barton gave her shelter at the Red Cross Hostel the night before she went out to the Spanish lines. Vancouver *Daily News Advertiser*, 23 Aug. 1914, 8.
56. *Mail and Empire*, 2 July 1898, Part 2, 4.
57. National Archives of the United States, Records of the Military, RG 107, Records of the Office of the Secretary of War, General Correspondence, File No. 5636, note from the Assistant Secretary of War to the Secretary of the Navy, dated 21 July 1898.
58. National Archives of the United States, Records of the Military, Bureau of Naval Personnel, RG 24, Box No. 64, "Niagara" Ship's Log Book, entry dated 22 July 1898.
59. *Mail and Empire*, 8 Aug. 1898, 1. Both Anna Benjamin and Mrs. Trumbull White got to Cuba a month earlier, before Santiago fell. Brown, *The Correspondents' War*, 212.
60. *Mail and Empire*, 8 Aug. 1898, 1.
61. Ibid., 2 Apr. 1910, 21. See also clipping from the *Winnipeg Telegram*, 11 June 1906, 4. PAC K.B.C. Papers, Vol. 3, File 1, Scrapbook. It is possible she wrote more romantically of her exploits as time passed. When she was actually in Cuba, she mentioned wandering around Santiago alone at night, dressed in her usual female garb, and of

riding "sideways on a man's saddle" in the hills outside the city. *Mail and Empire*, 31 July 1898, Part 2, 4.

62. David F. Trask, *The War with Spain in 1898* (New York: Macmillan Publishing Co., Inc. 1981), 265.

63. "Cervera's Lost Battleships," *Mail and Empire*, 27 Aug. 1898, Part 2, 4. Photo is in G.J.A. O'Toole, *The Spanish War—An American Epic-1898* (New York and London: W.W. Norton and Company 1984), 261 (author's private collection).

64. "The Pedlar's Pack," *Canada Monthly*, February 1915, 249.

65. *Mail and Empire*, 3 Sept. 1898, Part 2, 4.

66. Ibid., 10 Sept. 1898, Part 2, 4. Historians have since been quite critical of the U.S. government and military. See, for example, Foner, Vol. II, Ch. XV.

67. *Mail and Empire*, 7 Jan. 1905, 18. See also "Kit's Column," Vancouver *News Advertiser*, 23 Aug. 1914, 8.

68. "Kit's Column," Hamilton *Herald*, 12 Sept. 1914, 8.

69. *Mail and Empire*, 10 Sept. 1898, Part 2, 4.

70. Ibid., 24 Sept. 1898, Part 2, 4. See also undated clipping from the *Winnipeg Tribune* 11 June 1906, n.p. in PAC K.B.C. Papers, Vol. 3, File 1, Scrapbook.

71. Response to "Adhah," *Mail and Empire*, 5 Nov. 1898, Part 2, 8.

72. Response to "Pictures," Ibid., 22 Oct. 1898, Part 2, 8.

73. Response to "Eleanor," Ibid., 18 May 1907, 18.

74. Response to "M.E.R.," Ibid., 27 Oct. 1898, Part 2, 8.

75. "The Flaneur," Ibid., 20 Aug. 1898, Part 2, 6.

76. "Woman's Kingdom," Ibid., 25 Feb. 1899, Part 2, 4.

77. The *Mail and Empire* apparently issued a picture of her—one copy of which she saw on a factory wall, decorated with facial hair and a fez. Ibid., 27 May 1899, 17.

78. Ibid., 26 May 1900, pp. 16-17.

79. Ibid., 27 May 1899, 17.

80. She was referring to her out of pocket expenses. The man in question was probably W.J. Douglas. Undated letter (circa 1911) to Katherine Hale, former literary editor of the *Mail and Empire*, from Kathleen Blake Coleman. Hale-Garvin Papers, Lorne 2 Pierce Collection, 20016 B032f008, Queen's University, Kingston, Ontario.

81. Kit, *To London for the Jubilee*.

82. Response to "Gordon," *Mail and Empire*, 4 March 1899, Part 2, 4.

83. Ibid., 28 July 1900, 16. While she was in Key West, she complained of the heat and poor conditions endured in Tampa, commenting "malaria had laid hold of one." Ibid., 16 July 1898, Part 2, 4.

84. "Kit's Column," Hamilton *Herald*, 12 Sept. 1914, 8.

85. Gartshore-Waterous Interview.

CHAPTER 5

THE KINGDOM CHANGES

Kathleen married Doctor Theobald Coleman in Washington, D.C. on her way back from Cuba,[1] in what was probably a quiet, intimate ceremony. It took place on August 25, 1898 at St. John's, a small, Episcopal church, across Lafayette Square from the White House,[2] where fashionable Washington citizens and British Embassy officials attended Sunday services.[3]

With her usual reticence about her private life, Kit did not let her readers know about her marriage until two months later,[4] and even then, resisted their requests for details.[5] She did write that she had abandoned her earlier cynicism about love, that it brought her comfort and solace,[6] and she welcomed her "domestic peace" after her "hard experience" of life and all her travels. "There are not many things more sacred than wifehood and motherhood, little friend," she told "Jane."[7]

Despite her marriage, Kathleen continued to earn her own living, asserting in her private correspondence that she and her husband were not well off. Apparently the kind-hearted Doctor Coleman did not make much money because he did not like to charge his working-class patients.[8] Some years later, Kathleen confided to her colleague, Katherine Hale (Amelia Warnock)[9], that when management learned she had married, there were no good wishes or presents, only concern that their popular columnist might

A rare family photograph of Dr. Coleman and Kathleen on board ship, ca. 1902. (National Archives of Canada/PA 172137)

quit her job. "How could they lose one, pinched as we were!"[10]

It is not known whether or not her husband had any reservations about having a working journalist for a wife, but the marriage appeared to be happy.[11] Once Kit painted a cosy picture of "Himself," sitting with her in her den, puffing contentedly on his pipe as she read some of her correspondence out loud.[12] Despite the popular consensus against married women working outside the home,[13] she supported total economic independence for them, because it was not wise to be financially dependent on one's husband:

> Such dependence is the foundation of most of the tragedy of woman's lot—the economic dependence which makes marriage the one means left to a woman for getting the dinner she eats and the bed on which she lies. Thank God—the day is here when women are realizing this...Happiest of all is the woman who can turn her hand to something that will bring her in a little money for her personal use, for the children or herself. It doesn't hurt the man and it helps the woman.[14]

After the marriage, there were a number of changes in the "Kingdom." In the interests of family privacy, Kit all but dropped her anecdotes about her children because schoolmates were teasing them.[15] She was particularly protective of Patsy, who had begun writing for the *Mail and Empire*'s "Children's Corner" every Saturday, at first with her mother's encouragement.[16] When readers claimed the work was really Kit's, she decided that her daughter was too young to be in the public eye,[17] although she later changed her mind again.[18] In her own column, she still mentioned Thady and Patsy occasionally—she was proud, for example, of their prowess at school[19]—and in a rare moment of candour, even described Doctor Coleman as "the kindest of men and the children's only father now—and the best."[20] But she concentrated most of her maternal attention on the "Jungle People,"[21] the family pets, especially her Blue Bedlington Terriers, "Toby" and his mate "Gypsy," which she bred and successfully showed.[22]

After her marriage, Kit took on a double workload, being responsible for both her own weekly page and the family housekeeping. She often had to go without domestic help and did her chores between answers to scores of her correspondents,[23] a schedule which left her "often tired"[24] and always busy, "… scratching away with a pencil, at home or in the office, called hither and thither, now to the telephone, now to the kitchen, now to the attic, again to the cellar."[25] She was also trying to rework her Dickens' sketches[26] and had started writing an Irish novel,[27] which she said would probably never come out because time spent on "Woman's Kingdom" and "also the big house" prevented her from writing it.[28] The novel was the closest thing she ever attempted to an autobiography.[29] Several years later, during one of her depressions, she told "Sunbeam" that she didn't want to write her own story because no one would be interested, it would be a "stupid" task and her life as an adult had been too unhappy.[30]

Even in the happiest of circumstances, Kit was essentially a solitary, sometimes morose, woman. One of her favourite themes in the "Kingdom" during this period was the aloneness of the "Ego," which could not be assuaged, even in marriage, because the naked truth about one's own soul was too frightening, even to one's self.[31]

Her marriage certainly curtailed her adventures. When the Boer War broke out, hundreds of Canadian volunteers signed up to go to South Africa to fight for England.[32] Kit thought about going off to war again, because, despite her settled life, she was beginning to be "restless and longing for the wild places."[33] She told her readers that her feelings were probably "unwomanly" and she must accept that "someone must do garrison duty, and it falls to the share of the women."[34] In fact, Kathleen's husband had not wanted her to go to Cuba before their marriage[35] and he probably opposed her going to South Africa after it.

Her marital and domestic duties must have made her feel restricted at times. Many years later, she wrote frankly to her newly married colleague, Katherine Hale: "How I've thought of you Katherine—now one of us—of that long procession of *silent* women who give all into the man's hands and never afterwards speak—Marriage makes a woman dumb."[36]

Her own marriage changed her life drastically in another way. Kit, the world traveller used to roaming big cities and seeing exotic places, soon found herself writing the "Kingdom" from Copper Cliff, a remote mining town in northern Ontario, where the family moved after her husband had been hired as the company doctor.[37] The adolescent Thady, who had completed a business course,[38] went to work in a local bank[39] while Patsy was still at school down south.[40]

The development of Copper Cliff was part of the current economic trend in Canada. The mineral and other resources of New (northern) Ontario were considered particularly important, and American money and expertise were imported to develop it. In Copper Cliff, for example, the mines were run by the American-controlled Canadian Copper Company, based in Sudbury. The ore was mined, mixed and concentrated in northern Ontario, but sent to the Orford Company in New Jersey to be refined and sold.[41]

Copper Cliff was quite small and isolated. Kit was not sure that she would be able to endure life there,[42] unused as she was to the bleak conditions and her humble new home, which she vividly described for her readers:

> The queer frame house stands at the head of a gully. One half of it is painted a bright green. The other half is not painted at all. The kitchen is large enough for the stove—which is a good thing. The scenery—hills, rocks, stark black poles—the remains of trees sticking up everywhere, and sulphur smoke. As I write in a tiny room, the little house shakes and vibrates with the thunderous dynamite blastings... You have to draw your water from wells. Water, therefore, is almost as valuable as it was in Cuba. There are no bathrooms, therefore the big tin tub that has travelled more than half round the world, is again in requisition...It is cold with the clear, awful cold of the north and there are many journeys to the woodshed for coal and kindling.... Your hands harden

131

"Sailor Jim" (?) with Coleman family pets at their home in Copper Cliff, Ont. ca. 1903.   (National Archives of Canada/PA 172136)

into working condition as you go about your household work
(for there is no help to be got apparently) and the beautiful
brain-life seems to have given way to the purely physical and
material. [43]

She tried to cope professionally with her drastically curtailed horizons. When smallpox broke out in Copper Cliff,
she used her pages to urge vaccinations for all and
demanded that the local and provincial authorities set up
quarantine houses, [44] which they did. [45] Sometimes, she
helped her husband in his medical dispensary as "general
surgery attache"[46]—a role Kathleen and her daughter
played in real life, especially after Saturday night brawls
among the miners. [47] But it was difficult for her to come up
with fresh ideas for the "Kingdom" every week[48] and correspondence from her readers began to drop off. [49] Her problems were compounded by a series of illnesses[50] and
accidents—a burnt right hand[51], a fall down the basement
stairs, a sleigh mishap[52] and later, being thrown from her
horse. [53] Then her beloved "Toby" and "Gypsy" were poi-
soned by someone unknown. Kit reacted with deep sorrow
and anger, denying that they were guilty of chasing the
neighbours' hens. [54]

Her troubles depressed her, which took a toll on her self-
esteem as a journalist:

> Here I am, after all my "special" work, my trips abroad and
> to the wars—just dabbling away, doing the most ephemeral
> kind of work, simply because that's my limit and not being
> a "genius", I must just street car it in one rut all my life. [55]

But the traveller Kit had already reasserted herself and
she took trips, which she described for her readers, as often
as possible. She went to New York with Patsy, [56] on holiday
to Nantucket[57] and to dog shows in Toronto and St. Thomas,
Ontario, where "Toby's" and "Gipsy's" progeny won medals and ribbons. [58] She spent much of 1903 away in New York
and Jamaica. [59] She also had domestic help from the newly
graduated Patsy, who typed her copy, [60] bred the dogs[61] and
did the chores, [62] and from "Jim," an Irish sailor, who did

the heavy work[63] and entertained the family on the back steps with highly imaginative ghost stories.[64]

In 1904, the family finally left Copper Cliff to settle in Hamilton, just outside Toronto.[65] The mining company was probably just as glad to see them go, as both Kit and her husband were critical of it. She complained in print about government dependence on American resources in mineral exploration[66] and about the mining company's neglected upkeep on their home and the hospital.[67] After the family left, Doctor Coleman asked John Willison, editor of the Toronto *News*, for sympathetic coverage of the visit of Copper Cliff's mayor and his delegation to Toronto. In his letters, Coleman revealed that he did not like the American parent company's methods of running the Copper Cliff subsidiary and its unwillingness to pay medical insurance for its workers.[68]

The move out of Copper Cliff broadened Kit's horizons once again and she continued with her successful career. It was an era of lurid crime reporting in North America and, in 1904, she again earned front-page bylines when she "scooped" American and Canadian colleagues by getting an exclusive interview with Cassie Chadwick, a notorious, Canadian-born fraud artist, who was in jail in Cleveland.[69] Kit was also among the prominent women journalists covering the New York trial of the infamous Henry K. Thaw, who was accused of murdering his wife with the help of his beautiful mistress.[70] But Kit was happiest when she again got a rare opportunity to do the vivid, street-life reporting she used to love. In 1907 on another trip to England and Ireland, she spent a night disguised as a poor Irish woman, sleeping with the derelicts on the Thames Embankment in London.[71]

The real circumstances of her own life were, of course, quite different. Ever mindful of the power of social status, Kathleen continued to pull any strings she could to get her work done. She asked Prime Minister Laurier to arrange special press credentials giving her free access to the Canadian part of the International Exhibition in Dublin, in return for her writing up something flattering about him. "...may I have permission to ask for anything that might help you—and Canada?"[72]

But she was apparently not as strong and resilient as she was during her early travelling days. In Ireland, Kit reported, "I got a very sudden illness, a sharp attack of heart seizure since I came...but it is all over now."[73] The visit was a stressful one as it was the last time she saw her elderly mother or her beloved sister, then in hospital, alive.[74] From that time until she herself died eight years later, Kit often wrote about death and her own desire to "die with my harness on."[75] She did not want to depend on her children to take care of her and would "bitterly resent" being pensioned off.[76]

> Better far to go out while yet standing in the limelight, while yet believing in God and man, yet loving and being loved. Better far to leave the fire in its full and deep glow than live to sit by the hearth where only gray ashes crumble through the bars.[77]

Although the journalist wanted to keep on writing, it did not mean that she wanted to stay at the *Mail and Empire*. She had been unhappy there for some time because of the role party politics played in editorial decisions[78] and tried, unsuccessfully to leave.[79] She had been gradually enlisted into the newspaper's efforts to oust Liberal governments in Ottawa and at Queen's Park. Once, she roundly criticized her old acquaintance, Prime Minister Laurier, over his foreign investment policy.[80]

Kit claimed that she supported the Conservative party[81] but when the former editor of the Liberal Toronto *Globe*, John Willison, tired of pressure from his political bosses and started an independent paper, the Toronto *News*,[82] Kathleen unsuccessfully asked him for a job. She wanted "wider scope" in her work:

> An Independent Journal is just what Ontario wants. I dislike partyism immensely and in my small way I have tried for the broader, more generous effects. The narrowness of our press has always been a sore thing to me.[83]

Apparently, however, staffing arrangements for the *News* had already been made. Offering to freelance at space rates, she replied that she was not afraid to take on anything "under direction," adding, "thirteen years in a newspaper office knocks all the conceit out of one."[84]

That her own editor allowed Kit a political voice at all may have been a reflection of the public perception of the role women were playing in politics at the time. The idea that women held political power by domestic influence—but would not use a vote if they had it—had become a common one. It had replaced the Victorian argument that women were too weak to participate in political excitement.[85] But more changes were coming and Kit's own progression towards acceptance of suffrage for women roughly paralleled them.

Despite the best efforts of the Dominion Women's Enfranchisement Association, led by Dr. Augusta Stowe Gullen, and other groups, suffrage supporters had no success provincially or federally. While the professional and club women of Canada continued to be active and hone their organizational skills with social reforms, most did not see the vote for women as an issue as yet. Between 1893 and 1910, there were no bills in Parliament for women's suffrage.[86] Support from the National Council of Women of Canada did not come until 1910, because too many of its members—such as the WCTU and the Girls' Friendly Society—were too conservative. But by that time, the Dominion Women's Enfranchisement Association (later the Canadian Suffrage Association) and other suffrage groups had gained a foothold in the NCWC[87] and the earlier emphasis on maternalism as justification for women's involvement in social issues had given way to a broader and more pragmatic approach.[88]

At the same time, the United States also went through a period of the "doldrums" as far as the federal franchise was concerned, although there was some activity, mostly unsuccessful, in various states.[89] In Britain, the story was quite different. Despite the presence of conservative and moderate suffragists, public attention was drawn to the increasingly militant activities of the Suffragettes, whose leaders had first learned political strategy in the labour movement.[90] Conservative and radical women from both the United States and Britain visited Canada to talk about the importance of the vote for women.[91]

Kit was exposed to the work of female suffragists and social reformers through her growing connections with women journalists in Canada and abroad and particularly through the Canadian Women's Press Club, which she helped get started in 1904.[92] It was one of several, national groups formed by professional women in that period and many of its members were also connected with groups affiliated with the National Council of Women of Canada.[93] It is useful to examine Kit's role in the press club to better understand the evolving position of women in her profession and her acceptance of the suffrage movement later on.

Her trust of other press women had been building slowly. From the mid-1890s, she had begun to form a few friendships and, abandoning her suspicious attitude of earlier years, never hesitated to praise her colleagues generously in print. She described Katherine Hale, for example, as "...a really clever writer with the big human sympathy working all through her."[94] Hale, who had been appointed editor of the Saturday "Contemporary Literature" page,[95] had begun working on the *Mail and Empire* as a contributor, filling in for "the Queen," as she referred to Kit,[96] when the older woman fell ill with malaria and depression some time after returning from Cuba.[97]

When she could, Kit also encouraged talented female journalists she didn't even know, such as "B.D.T.," to whom she sent an unsolicited note praising the young woman's first published article. Kit had been "B.D.T.'s" girlhood idol. Her encouraging letter, full of "...the warm, brotherly, craftsmanlike appreciation that the writer's soul craved" had quite an impact on the young woman, who was stunned to see the famous signature at the bottom of the page.[98]

Kit was clearly impatient with the way in which most public relations and newspapermen snubbed their female colleagues, keeping them isolated in the profession. Canadian Pacific Railways, for example, had been taking train-loads of male journalists on free publicity jaunts to the Canadian west and other locales for years, but had never invited the women.[99] In a reply to a budding woman journalist, Kit underplayed her concern, but it was clear:

> I think we press women ought to get up a club or an association of some kind and try to meet once a year. I don't suppose we would claw each other too awfully and a little fun might be got out of our speech-making. Why should the Canadian men journalists have all the trips and banquets. Why, just whisper—neither "Katherine Hale" or "On Dit" or "Kit" have ever been invited to the Mail and Empire yearly banquet, and I think we might be let sit in a gallery or corner and watch the—the—oh, well—feed.[100]

Soon after, 19-year-old Margaret Graham of Montreal persuaded the C.P.R.'s publicity director, George Ham, to take sixteen women journalists on a free trip to the 1904 World Exposition in St. Louis, Missouri. The women's tour included veteran and "cub" members from across Canada. Aside from Graham and Kit, there were Sara McLagan, who had taken over as publisher of the Vancouver *World* when her husband died; George Ham's assistant, Kate Simpson Hayes, who had started as a children's columnist on the New Brunswick newspaper, *The St. Croix Courier*, thirty years before and Gertrude Balmer, the novice "Peggy" of the Woodstock, Ontario *Sentinel Review*. Robertine Barry, a former staff writer for *La Patrie*, who was publishing her own newspaper, *Le Journal de Francoise* in Montreal, was one of a strong French-Canadian contingent.[101] At Kit's suggestion, they formed the Canadian Women's Press Club to promote the personal and professional interests of its members, Canadian national sentiments in their work, and a higher standard of excellence in newspaper writing.[102] Not content with establishing a network of women journalists only in Canada, the CWPC affiliated with "United States women's

Kit at the centre of the Canadian Women's Press Club gathering, Winnipeg 1906. George Ham and Kate Simpson Hayes are on her left, Robertine Barry is second woman on her right. (W. Gibson/National Archives of Canada/PA 138845)

press clubs,''[103] and the Society of Women Journalists in Britain.[104]

At first, Kit, who was president, reported that there was little response to the news about the Canadian Women's Press Club, ''beyond the laughter of some of our 'gallant' male brethren of the pencil.''[105] Mainly with the help of Kate Simpson Hayes,[106] the club grew large enough to hold a national conference, in 1906 in Winnipeg, where western women, such as the prominent E. Cora Hind, had joined its ranks.[107]

Kit, who attended the conference with Patsy,[108] was very aware of the popular wisdom that strong-minded women were too competitive and jealous of one another to be able to work together as professionals. She hoped business could be conducted without rancour[109] and commented after their meeting was over: ''By the way, someone has interpreted C.W.P.C. to mean Cats With Pointed Claws, but I can assure you we kept them sheathed and wore gloves most of—not all—the time.''[110]

Although the club was supposed to be a professional support group, open only to women who earned their living by writing,[111] it did little to emphasize the journalistic or philosophical concerns of its members,[112] especially controversial ones. Most of its members did not report, for example, Kit's outspoken comments about missionaries in a speech she gave to the 1906 CWPC convention in Winnipeg. She believed that white missionaries should not impose their religion on people of other cultures, a view that angered several people in the audience, including an Archdeacon who stormed out, and several missionary society members.[113]

Many of the press club members took humble pride in their women's pages, with their fashion hints, recipes and society news—this last being what one of the journalists later referred to as the ''dishwashing side'' of the women's page ''household.'' It was a chore, she wrote, which ''must be done well and dressed in the dignified clothing of words.''[114]

Not surprisingly, the CWPC was not taken seriously by male colleagues, who, at best, patronized the women. The Regina *Daily Standard* described the club as "a little band of loyal workers... the natural guardians of the ideals of home life," whose work provided decorative appeal to the more prosaic contents of the daily newspapers.[115] In 1909, just after the predominantly-male Canadian Press Association met in Toronto, Kit scolded it in print for not inviting the members of the CWPC "at least for afternoon tea."[116] The next year, the CPA not only invited the press women to its convention, it asked her to speak, an invitation she turned down on the grounds that she would have been too intimidated by the predominantly male gathering. Her proposal that the two organizations affiliate, however,[117] was accepted.[118]

By this time, Kit, who was still uncomfortable with women "en masse,"[119] had receded into the background as far as the official leadership of the CWPC was concerned.[120] She did not always appear at press club gatherings—and was surrounded by a sea of eager young faces when she did[121]—and the club itself was being run by journalists who were also active in various women's organizations affiliated with the National Council of Women of Canada. They included the Honorary President, Mary Agnes FitzGibbon ("Lally Bernard," "Fitz-Clare," "Citoyenne" of various publications), who was a member of the Women's Canadian Club and the NCWC[122]; Mrs. Willoughby Cummings, the former "SAMA" of the *Globe*, who was the NCWC's press convener[123] and Mrs. Sanford Evans, who had presided over the 1906 press club meeting in Winnipeg and was also active in the NCWC.[124]

Kit had been slowly working toward acceptance of the women's movement, although she would never be a joiner. In Ottawa in 1896, observing the head of the National Council of Women of Canada, Lady Aberdeen, seated in the House beside her husband, the Governor-General, Kit began to see suffrage as inevitable but not a goal at that time for most women.[125] She was by that time aware, too, that most of the Canadian and American women in the cause, such as the conservative and socially prominent members of the Daughters of the American Revolution in Washington, who included her friend Mary Lockwood, were respectable, middle-class, intelligent and hardworking and that she couldn't dismiss them all as mannish and shrill.[126] Kit began to question her own hard line against "platform women." "Perhaps I argued from false premises."[127] But she did not believe that the women's rights movement would have any lasting effect on the relations between men and women, relations which, on one occasion, she denounced with unusual bitterness:

> Not all the "new" women in the world can alter the state of things; the human beasts of burden have always been the women. Women may talk and strive and revolt, but selfishness is so sown in the very flesh and blood and skin of man that it would take eons and any amount of cathartics to eliminate it.[128]

Her reluctance to actually endorse the vote may also have had something to do with news reports from Britain about the members of the Women's Social and Political Union, known as the Suffragettes, and the increasingly militant tactics they employed to win the vote for women. The historian, Andrew Rosen, has observed that Christabel Pankhurst, the leader of the WSPU, had quickly learned about the news value of militancy.[129] By 1906, the Suffragettes had gone from heckling politicians at public meetings—behaviour quite outside of Victorian mores for women[130]—to the even more radical tactic of forcing their way into Westminster and accosting MPs there.[131] Kit was aware of the growing agitation among women—especially in Britain—and was uneasy: "What is it women want? The unrest of them is frightful—and ominous."[132] She was not the only one who was nervous. In order to avoid any appearance of militancy, the National Council of Women of Canada, had, at its 1906 conference, rescinded an earlier motion in favour of suffrage. Kit heartily approved, preferring their reticence to visions of NCWC members "clawing the police in the lobby of the Ottawa House and being ejected screaming hysterically."[133]

Kit's colleague, Katherine Hale, was kinder. She visited London after the Suffragettes, frustrated by being thwarted by politicians, had taken to throwing rocks, with resulting arrests and hunger strikes by the imprisoned women.[134] Although the *Mail and Empire's* coverage was critical,[135] Hale wrote that the Suffragettes—as Cromwell in his time— were "driven to excess" in order to bring about revolution: "... women have always had to manoeuvre or fight so desperately for just the bare right of things."[136]

Kit's readers got in on the discussion as well. When the journalist insisted that women wielded their political influence at home,[137] she was challenged by "Suffragette Sympathizer," who reminded her that "...power divorced from responsibility is always dangerous..." and that women might influence husbands and sons to vote as they did, especially on moral issues, rather than the other way round. Kit did not reply.[138]

In the meantime, support for suffrage had been growing in Canada and the political debates became more heated. In 1909, the Canadian Suffrage Association, the WCTU and other groups presented a pro-suffrage petition of 100,000 signatures to the Ontario government.[139] Support was also growing among many progressive Protestant clergymen, the liberal press, farm groups and the unions and by 1912, there were eight pro-suffrage groups in Toronto.[140] Conservative church leaders, however, were still preaching that suffrage was a "Reform Against Nature" and that "Woman's Place is in the Home," sermons that were given prominent coverage in the newspapers.[141]

In the meantime, the Canadian Women's Press Club affiliated with the National Council of Women and planned its 1909 conference to coincide with that of the International Councils of Women.[142] The ICW conference involved women from all over the world, involved in every conceivable social reform movement. Kit appeared to be genuinely moved by what she saw and heard at the "womanly" and "dignified" gathering:

> One to be taken seriously, thoughtfully, earnestly and thank-
> fully by every woman who values all that makes life worth
> living for women, wifehood, maternity, household econom-
> ics, hygiene, the care of the children and the home, the mak-
> ing of laws and adjustment of them for the safeguarding of
> women and children, the better education, the better wage,
> the fairer hours, and in every way the uplift in life, the
> onward movement, the banner with Excelsior writ large upon
> it—the cheer, the comfort, the wide and tender sympathy...
> Magnificent, I call it. No smaller word will fit the work.[143]

The *Mail and Empire* gave the conference prominent news coverage[144] but tended to underscore the problems the delegates were having in agreeing over international peace issues,[145] the vote and women's work.[146] For example, British novelist Edith A. Barnett's contention that professional women, childless by choice, were leaving their homes behind was included in an inside page story but quoted in a glaring headline on page one. A contrary response from a New York physician, Doctor Rosalie Morton, was given one paragraph at the end of the same story.[147] When Lady Aberdeen took the floor and declared herself in favour of suffrage, the newspaper criticized her, declaring that women had all the power they would ever need in the home and did not need to seek it in the polling booth.[148]

After the Congress, Kit gave space in the "Kingdom" to women who argued both sides of the suffrage cause. In September, she ran a plea from the leading Canadian suffragist, Flora MacDonald Denison, who argued that the vote was a basic human right and was part of the responsibilities women must fulfill for themselves and their children.[149] Kit also ran a letter from an unnamed anti-suffrage reader, who scolded her for running the Denison letter and "philandering with the subject of the vote for women." Here, the journalist revealed for the first time that her newspaper's editorial policy on suffrage could affect what she herself wrote: "... Woman's Kingdom will not champion the cause of Woman Suffrage—unless so ordered by the powers that be."[150]

Soon afterwards, however, she wrote long articles about two early champions of education for women, Mary Astell and Mary Wollenstonecraft, noting in the second article that when married women were treated in law as men's chattel, it was no wonder that they wanted the vote.[151]

Then, Emmeline Pankhurst, Christabel's mother and co-leader of the British Suffragettes, was invited to visit Toronto. While militancy was not embraced as a tactic by Canadian women, many of them admired and sympathized with Mrs. Pankhurst and her colleagues.[152] Kit urged her readers to go and hear the Englishwoman present her case as a "gentlewoman" of "fine intellect" who deserved a "respectful hearing."[153]

Her urging ran contrary to her own newspaper, which warned its readers against Mrs. Pankhurst. The Suffragette leader was very skilled at addressing and holding a crowd,[154] but the newspaper accused her of being an autocrat who denied members in her own association a vote in its proceedings and told readers not to be fooled by her appearance and manner.[155] Nonetheless, the *Mail and Empire* gave her talks in Toronto prominent coverage and reported that many of the thousands of people who attended them had been "converted."[156] One of the those most impressed by her appearance and manner was Kit:

> With all her grace, her magnetism, her fragility, and that spiritual light upon her face, Mrs. Pankhurst reminded me of nothing so much as a human skyscraper—a slender structure with nerves of steel—the sort of structure that in architecture would withstand fire and earthquake, that in human form will withstand every sort of persecution, and, for the sake of a cause, face with utter calmness, death itself.[157]

The journalist liked the logic of the Suffragette leader's arguments and her explanation of the conditions under which British women lived: "There is sound reason in favour of her argument to give votes to women," she wrote,[158] although she never did condone the violence of

145

Kathleen Blake Coleman, aged about 50. ca. 1906.
(National Archives of Canada/PA 172135)

some of their tactics.[159] Shortly afterwards, Kit finally revealed herself as being in favour of suffrage:

> ... I shall welcome it for women, for I believe it to be the best thing in the end for them and the race, but I am not a Suffragist, or rather, worker in the cause. I most thoroughly admire the Canadian women who are earnest in the movement but it does not att (obliterated—probably "attract me") personally—a small matter, my friend, and one wholly personal.[160]

The following week, she told her readers that she would vote Conservative in the next provincial election.[161]

It is not exactly clear why her public stance changed. Mrs. Pankhurst's appearance may have been a factor,[162] but it was more likely Kit's growing awareness of women's solidarity. Her involvement with the press club had taught her how to work more closely with women and she had observed first hand the various movements for suffrage and other social reforms. The old rivalries and jealousies between women were fading, she noted; they were more supportive of each other. "Nothing is more significant of the advance of woman along broadening lines than the disappearing of the harsh attitude of woman towards woman."[163]

She still refused to become involved in the movement herself, not just because of her personal preferences[164]—but as a reflection of the trend towards "objectivity" in journalism in general.[165] She told a young writer, who was apparently torn between the demands of her work and her feminism, that the two didn't mix:

> Suffragette—The editor who essays the role of a practical politician while remaining in his editorial chair generally makes a botch of both vocations. You cannot do two things well at the one time. My advice would be to cut out one or the other.[166]

Kit herself reacted furiously to any attempts by suffragists and feminists to co-opt her or make her a figurehead in the cause. When Flora MacDonald Denison, in one of her regular Toronto *Sunday World* columns, wrote about her as an example of a woman who was able to make her way in a man's world despite opposition, Kit responded by going out of her way to lie about her experiences. She quoted the offending column at great length, interjecting her denials.

Denison somewhat inaccurately claimed that Kit was able to make the same salary as men who were supporting families and do her own housecleaning and child-rearing as well: "Kit did all these things, possibly easing her conscience by the thought that though a journalist, she was still a real, true woman."[167] Kit responded that this was "...a touch of satire unworthy of Mrs. Denison, who at times, appears to be obsessed by the Suffrage issue..." and insisted that she worked in order to have a home, and that her home had always come first. She claimed she was not, as Denison wrote, ever accused of doing men's work, and seemed to forget that male colleagues had tried to keep her out of Cuba and snubbed her at professional gatherings:

> Never, in all my life as a journalist, did I ever receive from any man of my acquaintance in my office or my home, the faintest suggestion that in earning my living, and that of my children, I was overstepping the limit of womanhood or taking any man's place. I made my own place, and met always and ever the kindest help and recognition from the newspaper men who were my comrades and brothers. If any objection came it was invariably from the other sex.[168]

To Denison's observation that journalistic work had left Kit little time or opportunity to be the success she should have been in the literary world, Kit, omitting the fact that she had herself made the same complaint, replied that she had the time, but not the ability.[169]

In fact, after her health had begun to fail, Kit appeared to come to terms with the fact that she would never be a leading literary figure. Her youthful dreams of fame had led to a great deal of depression because they were not being fulfilled, she wrote, depressions during which she had not just "blue" days but "whole weeks of indigo." Now she could look on the world through rose-coloured glasses:

> But, oh, how good, to have outlived all that, to have discovered one's limitations—(fence round a yard-wide

garden)—to have been brow-beaten and humiliated, and fashioned from a Brobdinagian to a Lilliputian![170]

But her greatest professional crisis was still to come—her unhappy parting from the *Mail and Empire*. It started with management's decision to drop her correspondence column, a decision taken while Kit was away touring England with Canadian and British journalists in the autumn of 1910.[171] She and her readers fought the decision, but to no avail.[172] She continued to write the "Kingdom," but, instead of answers to her letters, she was producing a short, daily column, first called "Kit's Corner" and then "Kit's Comments." It consisted of a few paragraphs, covering light topics of interest, much like her Pot-Pourri section in the "Kingdom," but it was buried near the classified ads.[173] That Kit was not happy with the state of affairs is evident by the way she discussed her profession in one of the last columns she wrote for the *Mail and Empire*:

> Of all lines of work it is one of the hardest, most hurried, least encouraged and ungrateful in returns. And yet, we men and women, who have toiled and sweated at it—love it! ... And yet—for a little peace!—for one—even one— holiday where the soul would not be taking notes—consciously or unconsciously—where the burden of work to come would not be bearing to the earth with its weight the little happy days of joy![174]

In her letter to Katherine Hale, who had also apparently left the *Mail and Empire* on bad terms, she commented: "God! it makes the gorge rise in one! the way they treat us—these Corporations!"[175]

Suddenly, in February 1911, there was no "Kit's Comments" and her signature had disappeared from the "Kingdom."[176] A few months later, in her new syndicated column, she explained that she had quit the *Mail and Empire* because she found both the "Kingdom" and the daily column too much work.[177] She had tried to tell her readers that she was leaving, but the *Mail and Empire*, with an eye to its circulation figures, had edited her goodbye out of the final column.[178]

Kathleen had apparently tried without success to get a job on the Toronto *Globe* before striking out on her own. She asked Sir Wilfrid Laurier to arrange it, adding in a second note, "...it would be much better if I did not appear as having asked your favour in this regard." He complied, but was told that the *Globe* already had three women on staff who supplied it with enough material. The possibility of hiring her had earlier been discussed but not pursued. No reason was given. [179]

Once her freelance career was underway, however, Kit seemed to enjoy it more than her old job on the *Mail and Empire*. [180] She found it an exhilarating challenge, if not a very profitable one:

> That is the Irish of it, rather a splendid feeling that you will
> have to wrest fresh coins from the crest of such lucky waves
> as come lifting and lowering that frail craft of yours which
> is named "My Business Life." A joke of a craft, between you
> and me, with the touch of a pirate in her. [181]

Aside from the syndicated column, she also resurrected the male voice of "The Pedlar" for her women's feature in *Canada Monthly*, which she wrote as "Kit." In that column, she dealt with topics that interested her at greater length. Her first "Pedlar's Pack," for example, included her comments on an interview with Sarah Bernhardt, the last days of Tolstoy, cruelty to animals, the Crippen murder in England and whether or not women had a sense of humour. [182]

The life of a freelance writer did not give her as much editorial freedom as one might expect. Among the newspapers in which her column appeared were the conservative Ottawa *Evening Journal*, the pro-Liberal Stratford *Daily Beacon*, [183] the independent Hamilton *Herald*, the business-minded Vancouver *News-Advertiser* and the populist, pro-labour Toronto *Sunday World*. Prudently, Kit did not declare herself for one political party or another but indicated liberalism in most of her attitudes. When "Albert N." accused her of being a socialist, she replied: "Yes, in a conservative way.

Socialism means equality of opportunity to my mind."[184] She could be sardonic about the role of business in Canada's political life but candidly told her readers that she could risk writing only so much about it: "(I have to make my living by this scribbling and daren't get to cracking heads with my shillelaghs in a political or religious melee.)"[185]

But the First World War changed that. Kit became far more outspoken, especially in matters of religious faith and tolerance toward the enemy. Despite her occasional sermons on God and nature, she was not a "creedist"[186] and admitted that she had always counselled faith in her columns because she felt it was her duty to do so, despite her own many spiritual questions.[187] Now she adopted a new conviction. She began to warn her readers that the world conflict was a sign of the advent of Armageddon.[188]

It is not clear why she believed this. It may have had something to do with various upheavals in her private life. Her son had contracted tuberculosis,[189] she herself had been gravely ill and close to death during the summer of 1913,[190] and her daughter, who had been her right hand,[191] had recently married and she missed her.[192] But she was also likely overwhelmed by the onset of the most terrible war the world had yet seen.[193]

Because of pressure from editors, Kit wrote a lot that was not critical about the First World War,[194] but what she wrote may still have been too liberal for many of them. When she received letters abusing the Germans, she declared that no side was innocent of atrocities and that lack of compassion, especially for enemy women, who were very like Canadian and British ones, did no one any good:

> Were I a German Frau, instead of happily being an Irish Canadian woman, I would stand up as bravely as I could for my country and my people...We have every reason to be charitable, and none at all to be abusive. Some one writes to me, "You can be too broadminded, Kit." But can you? Perhaps in younger days one would have felt more of the brutality and fierceness of war stirring in one. But Time gentles the primeval savage in us all... You are enabled to slip into the shoes of the German women, or the French, or the

Kathleen's third husband, Doctor Theobald Coleman, ca. 1917.
(National Archives of Canada/PA 172134)

> Belgian. And for each—if one bit of god-head remains in you,
> you must feel compassion and pity.[195]

But Kit's defence of enemy women, coupled with the demand for more newspaper space for war news,[196] may have cost her. The following week, her readers found only a cryptic note:

> A shell—German—has hit KIT'S COLUMN. It is smashed to smithereens. But before I go I have something to say to you. It is this: All along I have tried to be decent and charitable and square in my writings. I have felt that there is nothing like the broad mind—the wide eye. The underdog always made his appeal. But now, today, my last word. Would to God that I were a second Charlotte Corday. I would shoot the Kaiser in his throat. Kit.[197]

A few months later, in May 1915, Kathleen Blake Coleman died at home in Hamilton, after a bout of pneumonia, leaving behind her heart-broken husband,[198] her terminally ill son[199] and her daughter who, the year before, had given birth to a grand-child.[200]

Her last words as a journalist, published posthumously in *Canada Monthly* the following month, were a blunt plea against the moral hypocrisy that prompted people to ignore children sired out of wedlock by soldiers overseas. Kit described the "war babies" as "...the cruel outcome of our nonsensical wars, our absurd and shocking 'civilization,' our conventional mock modesty."[201] Her final message was characteristic of the journalist who, throughout her long career, had prided herself on her maternalism as much as her outspokenness.

Notes

1. Confusion about the datelines on her articles make it difficult to trace her exact movements at this time. Brown says "Kathleen Blake Watkins" was listed among the passengers arriving in New York 13 August 1898 in the following day's newspaper. Brown *The Correspondents' War*, 210. But her story about being confined to the "Comal" for several days after it reached Florida and the length of time it would take her to get to New York from there contradict Brown's account, especially if she went to Washington first. It is possible that she travelled from New York to Washington for her marriage on 25 Aug., perhaps prefering to be married privately, but in the presence of friends such as Mary Lockwood. In any event, she likely wrote up several of her Cuba articles on her way back from the war, rather than at the scene. See, for example, an article datelined Santiago 20 Aug., which appeared in the *Mail and Empire* 3 Sept. 1898, Part 2, 4.

2. The marriage certificate states that Kathleen was married only once before, giving credence to the family story that E.J. Watkins was a bigamist. Doctor Coleman, who was born at Seaforth, Ontario, was thirty-two; Kathleen's age was given as thirty-four (she was actually forty-two) and the marriage register gives both her father's and her name as Blake, not Ferguson. Records of the Marriage Bureau of the District of Columbia, Vol. 51, No. 5660; marriage register of St. John's Church, Lafayette Square, Washington, D.C., 25 Aug. 1898, entry No. 343.

3. Constance McLaughlin Green, *The Church On Lafayette Square 1815-1970* (Washington: Potomac Books Inc. 1970), pp. 63-65.

4. *Mail and Empire*, 16 Nov. 1898, Part 2, 4.

5. Response to "Homo," Ibid., 1 July 1899, 19.

6. Response to "Violet," Ibid., 2 Sept. 1899, 19.

7. Ibid., 27 May 1899, 17.

8. Ferguson, 3.

9. See Kit's reference to her in the Stratford *Daily Beacon*, 25 Nov. 1911, 9.

10. "Kit" to Katherine Hale, op. cit.

11. Gartshore-Waterous Interview.

12. "An Old Carpenter" wanted to know if she approved of men smoking. *Mail and Empire*, 15 July 1899, Part 2, 4.

13. For example, the National Council of Women of Canada supported the establishment of public nurseries for children, but still espoused a preference that mothers stay at home. Veronica Strong-Boag, *Parliament of Women*, pp. 251-252. Her children were almost

adolescents when Kathleen married Dr. Coleman, which might
have made a difference to her.

14. Response to "Arnold M.," *Mail and Empire*, 8 Aug. 1903, 19.
15. Ibid., 3 June 1899, 16.
16. "Children's Corner," Ibid., 23 Apr. 1898, Part 2, 5. One of the child's
essays, "Beauty," was written clearly with good imagery and apt
quotes from the poet, Shelley. An editor's note said it was published
as the child had written it in school and was shown to her mother
after it appeared in print. Ibid., 16 Apr. 1898, Part 2, 5.
17. Response to "Pansy Blossom," "Woman's Kingdom," Ibid., 5 Nov.
1898, Part 2, 8. For this reason, she had not allowed her daughter
to enter the *Mail and Empire's* 1898 Christmas competition for young
writers. Ibid., 8 Apr. 1899, 16.
18. Response to "Katie," Ibid., 1 July 1899, 19; Ibid., 23 Mar. 1901, 16;
Ibid., 7 Mar. 1903, 21.
19. Ibid., 15 July 1899, Part 2, 5.
20. Ibid., 31 Aug. 1901, 17. Her granddaughter, Kit Waterous, remem-
bers Dr. Coleman, who died 10 years after Kathleen, as a very kind
man who was loved by his step-children. Gartshore-Waterous
Interview.
21. Response to "Ethel," *Mail and Empire*, 3 Nov. 1901, 18.
22. Ibid., 2 June 1900, 17. Kennel Club registration forms for "Toby"
and "Gypsy" are in PAC K.B.C. Papers, Vol. 1, File 5.
23. *Mail and Empire*, 13 May 1899, 17. In December, 1900, she was facing
a work-basket containing 220 unanswered letters. Ibid., 15 Dec.
1900, 17.
24. Response to "Wexford," Ibid., 16 Sept. 1899, 17.
25. Response to "Psyche," Ibid., 17 Feb. 1900, 19.
26. Ibid., 27 Jan. 1900, 17. One version, a fragment of which still exists,
had a male protagonist wandering through Dickens' London. PAC
K.B.C. Papers, Vol. 2, File 3.
27. Response to "Canadian," *Mail and Empire*, 17 Feb. 1900, 18.
28. Response to "The Silent Scotchman," Ibid., 31 Mar. 1900, 19; and
Ibid., 14 Apr. 1900, Part 2, 5.
29. Parts of the manuscript are in PAC K.B.C. Papers, Vol. 2, Files 13-18.
30. *Mail and Empire*, 10 May 1902, 19.
31. Ibid., 5 Jan. 1907, 18.
32. Brown and Cook, *Canada 1896-1921*, pp. 38-42.
33. She couldn't resist writing about it as if she were really there and
supported a campaign to raise funds for a Canadian hospital ship,
which the Canadian government refused to supply. *Mail and Empire*,
13 Jan. 1900, 16; Ibid., 27 Jan. 1900, 16. At the same time, she disliked
the jingoism in Canada associated with the war. Response to "Mary
Brown-Smith," Ibid., 5 May 1900, 17.

34. Ibid., 6 Jan. 1900, 16. In an undated note scribbled on the back of one of her short story manuscripts, Kathleen told a Walter Wilkinson she had been hoping he would send her out with a contingent. Wilkinson had chosen a Mrs. Donald Shaw instead, who, Coleman insisted, wanted to plagiarize her copy from Cuba. It is not clear, however, whether this was during the Boer War or the First World War. K.B.C. Papers, Vol. 2, File 9, Mss. of "Ellen." Patsy Gartshore's notes on her mother refer to her ongoing disagreements with "Wilkinson." Ibid., File 38.
35. Gartshore-Waterous Interview.
36. Kit's emphasis. "Kit" to Katherine Hale, op. cit.
37. *Mail and Empire*, 16 Mar. 1901, 16. There are several photographs of the Coleman family in Copper Cliff. PAC K.B.C. Papers, 1987-148. LOC A-93.
38. Response to "Bog-Myrtle," *Mail and Empire*, 2 Feb. 1901, 17.
39. Response to "Moneira," 9 Feb. 1901, 17. Kit later wrote that she would not encourage mothers to let their sons work in banks where the pay for a cashier ranged between $250-$500 a year and the pay for a teller was $750. Hamilton *Herald*, 14 Sept. 1912, 7. Her real life son was, at one point, with the "Bank of Toronto" in London, Ontario. A contemporary remembered him there as a charming and generous young man, who was not very well off. Letter from Mrs. Robert (Mary) Hague to Mrs. John ("Patsy") Gartshore, postmarked 14 May 1953. PAC K.B.C. Papers, Vol. 4, File 4.
40. Response to "H.M.S.," *Mail and Empire*, 23 Feb. 1901, 16.
41. Brown and Cook, *Canada 1896-1921*, Chapter 5.
42. Responses to various correspondents, especially "M.I.F.," *Mail and Empire*, 9 Feb. 1901, pp. 16-17.
43. Ibid., 9 Feb. 1901, 16.
44. Ibid., 9 Mar. 1901, 16.
45. Ibid., 16 Mar. 1901, 16.
46. Response to "D.," Ibid., 5 Oct. 1901, 19.
47. Gartshore-Waterous Interview.
48. *Mail and Empire*, 8 Feb. 1902, 18.
49. Ibid., 3 May 1902, 19.
50. Ibid., 10 Aug. 1901, 16.
51. Ibid., 11 Jan. 1902, 18.
52. Ibid., 25 Jan. 1902, 18.
53. Ibid., 14 Nov. 1903, 20.
54. Ibid., 15 Mar. 1902, 18 and Ibid., 22 Mar. 1902, 18.
55. Response to "Isabelle," Ibid., 29 Nov. 1902, 19.
56. Ibid., 20 Apr. and Ibid., 27 Apr. 1901, pp. 18, 19.
57. Ibid., 23 Aug. 1902, 16.
58. Ibid., 4 Oct. 1902, 18.

59. Ibid., 21 Feb. 1903 and Ibid., 12 Sept. 1903, pp. 20.
60. Response to "Mollie Alanna," Ibid., 29 Aug. 1903, 20.
61. Response to "Ignorance," Ibid., 1 Jan. 1903, 18.
62. Ibid., 24 Jan. 1903, 19.
63. Ibid., 19 Dec. 1903, 18.
64. *Canada Monthly*, Vol. 12, No. 3 (July 1912), pp. 229-230. "Jim" was a real person, according to Kathleen's grandchildren. Gartshore-Waterous Interview. A photograph of a man fitting his description is among those in the Coleman family collection taken in Copper Cliff. PAC K.B.C. Papers, 1987-148 LOC A-93.
65. Response to "Anxious Enquirer," *Mail and Empire*, 17 June 1905, 20.
66. Ibid., 28 Nov. 1903, 18.
67. Ibid., 9 Jan. 1904, 18.
68. Dr. Theobald Coleman to John Willison, letters dated 5 and 19 Apr. 1905. PAC, John Willison Papers, Vol. 9, Folder 73.
69. *Mail and Empire*, 19 Dec. 1904, pp. 1-2; Ibid., 20 Dec. 1904, pp. 1-2 and "Woman's Kingdom", 24 Dec. 1904, 20.
70. Ibid., 2 Mar. 1907, 18; Ibid., 9 Mar. 1907, 18. Her criticisms of her female colleagues' "sob sister" copy apparently angered several of them, who argued they were forced to write sentimental stories by their editors. See the Hamilton *Herald*, 13 July 1912, 7. See also Marzolf, 37.
71. *Mail and Empire*, 2 Nov. 1907, 21.
72. Laurier wrote to a Mr. Hutchinson of the Canadian exhibition and sent a letter to Lady Aberdeen—then in Ireland—who invited Kathleen to lunch. The three letters are in PAC K.B.C. Papers, Vol. 1, Files 4, 3.
73. Response to "S.E.G.," *Mail and Empire*, 7 Sept. 1907, 23.
74. Ibid., 5 Oct. 1907, 24; response to "A Remote Village," Ibid., 20 Nov. 1909, 21.
75. Response to "Dora (Vancouver)," Hamilton *Herald*, 19 Oct. 1912, 7.
76. *Mail and Empire*, 10 Aug. 1907, 22.
77. Ibid., 30 Nov. 1907, 20.
78. The *Mail and Empire's* management included editor-in-chief Arthur Wallis, a Conservative who was a strong believer in party newspapers, and W. Sanford Evans, a prominent party activist. See "The Editors of the Leading Canadian Dailies," in *Canadian Magazine*, February 1899, (Vol. XII, No. 4), 346.
79. In 1900, she had asked Prime Minister Laurier for an unspecified job with the Ministry of Agriculture, but he had none to offer. Letter from Laurier dated 20 March 1900 addressed to her residence at 569 Spadina Avenue, Toronto. PAC K.B.C. Papers, Vol. 1, File 4.
80. *Mail and Empire*, 15 Oct. 1904, 18.

81. Response to "North Pole or Stony Lake," Ibid., 7 May 1904, 21.
82. Rutherford, *A Victorian Authority*, pp. 222-224. See also John Willison, *Reminiscences Political and Personal* (Toronto: McClelland 1919).
83. "Mrs. Blake Coleman" (signed "Kit") to John Willison Dec. 1902. PAC John Willison Papers, Vol. 9, Folder 73.
84. Ibid. Earlier, Kit had asked Willison to accept one of her Irish stories. Letter from "Mrs. Blake Coleman" (signed "Kit") to Willison, 1 Oct. 1899. The *News* preferred syndicated copy for the women's page. See letter to Willison from another female applicant, F.B.M. Collier of Orangeville, Ontario, 17 April 1905. PAC John Willison Papers, Vol. 9, Folder 73.
85. Cleverdon, pp. 5-7.
86. Ibid., pp. 25-28. As late as 1911, only 11.8 per cent of readers polled by the Montreal *Star* favoured the vote for women. Cited by Veronica Strong-Boag, *Parliament of Women*, 276, fn 120. A Canadian writer noted, at the time, that privileged, upper-class women in Canada consistently opposed suffrage. Laura E. McCully, "The Woman Suffrage Movement of Canada," *Canada West Magazine*, April 1909, 374.
87. Veronica Strong-Boag, *Parliament of Women*, 100.
88. Ibid., 280.
89. Flexner, *Century of Struggle*, 248.
90. Rosen, pp. 20-23.
91. Cleverdon, 16.
92. Freeman, "'Every Stroke Upward'," op. cit. Before the Canadian Women's Press Club was established, Kit mentioned that she was "vice-president for the Canadian presswomen" in some international press organization which she did not name. *Mail and Empire*, 31 Aug. 1901, 17. It may have been the International Press Union of Women Journalists, whose president, Mary Lockwood, had helped her in Cuba.
93. Strong-Boag, *Parliament of Women*, 110.
94. Response to "Kathia Maiden," *Mail and Empire*, 31 Aug. 1901, 17.
95. "Contemporary Literature," Ibid., 17 Oct. 1900, 17.
96. "Woman's Kingdom," Ibid., 4 Aug. 1900, Part 2, 4.
97. Ibid., 28 July 1900, 16.
98. Note on Kit by "B.D.T.," *Canada Monthly*, June 1915, 104. "Women's Kingdom" always ended with a facsimile of Kit's signature.
99. George Ham, *Reminiscences of a Raconteur* (Toronto: Musson 1925), pp. 152-153.
100. "On Dit" was the newspaper's unsigned society column. Response to "Mabel Black," *Mail and Empire*, 28 May 1904, 18.

101. PAC Media Club of Canada, Vols. 17, 18 and 23. See also Freeman, "'Every Stroke Upward'," op. cit. The number of women journalists was growing in Quebec as it was elsewhere. The Clio Collective, *Quebec Women—A History*, in Roger Gannon and Rosalind Gill, (trans.) (Toronto: The Women's Press 1987). pp. 176-180; 224.

102. The early version apparently referred to the social and moral connections of press club members but, according to the first printed annual report, this was later deleted. No reason was given. PAC Media Club of Canada, Vol. 1. 1907-1908 Annual Report, Constitution, 6.

103. Probably the International Press Union of Women Journalists. PAC K.B.C. Papers, Vol. 4, File 2. Clipping from the *Western British American*, 25 June 1904 (n.p.).

104. PAC Media Club of Canada, Vol. 1, 1907-1908 Annual Report, 16. British women were also having trouble being accepted in the journalism profession, according to an article written in London for the *Mail and Empire*, 2 Apr. 1904, 18.

105. Response to "Alleluia," Ibid., 9 July 1904, 18. The CPR's publicity director, George Ham, had been made an honorary member of the CWPC for his role in helping it get started. He was the only male. PAC Media Club of Canada, Vol. 1. 1907-1908 Annual Report.

106. Response to "H.H.," *Mail and Empire*, 11 Feb. 1905, 18. Simpson Hayes moved to Winnipeg where she wrote as "Mary Markwell" of the Manitoba *Free Press*.

107. The membership came to number about 50 by 1908. PAC Media Club of Canada Vol. 1. 1907-1908 Annual Report, membership list. Hind, the agriculture editor of the *Manitoba Free Press*, became world-renowned for the accuracy of her crop forecasts. Kennethe Haig, *Brave Harvest* (Toronto: Thomas Allen 1945).

108. As "Patricia" of the *Hamilton Herald*. The trip was for journalists only and she applied for the job in order to be able to accompany her mother. *Mail and Empire*, 7 July 1906, 20 and Gartshore-Waterous Interview.

109. Undated clipping on the opening of the CWPC's first annual meeting, 1906. Winnipeg *Bulletin*, Scrapbook, PAC K.B.C. Papers, Vol. 3, File 1.

110. *Mail and Empire*, 30 June 1906, 20.

111. PAC Media Club of Canada, Vol. 1. 1907-1908 Annual Report, Constitution, Article 5, 6. The policy meant that women such as Canadian suffrage leader Flora MacDonald Denison, who later wrote a left-leaning weekly newspaper column for the Toronto *World*, but made her living as a dressmaker, would not be eligible for membership in the CWPC. See Gorham, "Flora MacDonald

Denison," op. cit. The CWPC membership lists made no mention of any women affiliated with labour newspapers. PAC Media Club of Canada, Vol. 1, Annual and Triennial Reports.

112. CWPC Annual and Triennial Reports were carefully worded as a rule. Ibid. Strong-Boag notes that, despite its vaunted aims, the CWPC's activities appeared to be mostly social. Strong-Boag, *Parliament of Women*, pp. 110-112. See also various accounts of the 1906 CWPC trip through the Rockies which stressed social events. Various clippings in Scrapbook, PAC K.B.C. Papers, Vol. 3, File 1; CWPC gag newspaper *Sunset News Bulletin*, 1906, in Ibid., general files (horizontal storage). See also Effie Storer's scrapbook, Vol. 23; microfilm C-4474; and "Woman's Kingdom," *Mail and Empire*, 9 June, 16 June, 25 June, 30 June 1906, pp. 20.

113. "E.G.K." in "The Woman's Quiet Hour" column, *The Western Home Monthly*, July 1906, 35. In a column in which Kit recalled the Winnipeg incident, she repeated her views. *Canada Monthly*, Vol. 12, No. 6, Oct. 1912, pp. 471-472.

114. Florence Sherk ("Gay Page" of the Fort William, Ontario *Herald*), in PAC Media Club of Canada, Vol. 1. 1910-1913 Triennial Report, 10.

115. PAC K.B.C. Papers, Vol. 3, File 1, Scrapbook, clipping, n.d., n.p.

116. *Mail and Empire*, 27 Mar. 1909, 20. The CPA's 1908 membership list contains six female names out of roughly 400 members. At least two of these women were also CWPC members. Canadian Press Association, *A History of Canadian Journalism* (Toronto: Canadian Press Association 1908, rev. 1958).

117. *Mail and Empire*, 28 May 1901, 22.

118. PAC Media Club of Canada, Vol. 1. 1909-1910 Annual Report, 7.

119. Response to "Menteuse," *Mail and Empire*, 3 July 1909, 21.

120. It appears to have been her own choice. She wrote that her sister members dubbed her "The Lonely Lady of Grosvenor Square." Response to "David Copperfield," *Mail and Empire*, 23 Apr. 1910, 23. It may also have had to do with her poor health and her depressions, which continued. She learned self-hypnosis to help herself feel better. Response to Mrs. "M.E.P.," Ibid., 5 Feb. 1910, 20.

121. Note on Kit by "B.D.T.," *Canada Monthly*, June 1915, 104. See also the effusive letter about Kit addressed to "Katherine," dated 12 April 1934, from Gertrude Balmer Watt, PAC K.B.C. Papers, Vol. 2, File 37 and two clippings: "'Kit' Beloved by Thousands Passes Away in Hamilton," by "Helen Ball," Toronto *News*, n.d., n.p., and "Kit Has Written Her Last Copy," by "Cornelia," Toronto *Telegram*, 17 May 1915, 20 in PAC K.B.C. Papers, Vol. 2, Files 30-33, reprinted in Burkholder, "Kit," copy in File 34.

122. PAC Media Club of Canada, Vol. 18, Mary Agnes Clare FitzGibbon's file; Amy Ridley, "The Dual Struggle: Mary Agnes FitzGibbon, Toronto Journalist," M.A. Research Essay, Institute of Canadian Studies, Carleton University, 1983.
123. *Mail and Empire*, 16 June 1909, 7.
124. Ibid., 14 July 1906, 20. Her husband was an MP from Winnipeg and a member of the *Mail and Empire's* editorial board. Ibid., 19 June 1909, 20 and "The Editors of the Leading Canadian Dailies," 346, op. cit.
125. *Mail and Empire*, 9 May 1896, 5.
126. Lockwood was a director of both the Daughters of the American Revolution and the General Federation of Women's Clubs. See "Big Federation Convention," *New York Times*, 3 July 1898, 12; also the *General Federation Clubwoman*, Sept. 1898, 184 and March 1900, 260. In fact, the women's suffrage movement had been "respectable" in the United States from the 1880s. Flexner, pp. 216-218.
127. *Mail and Empire*, 4 Mar. 1899, Part 2, 4.
128. Ibid., 3 Aug. 1907, 22.
129. Rosen, 53.
130. Ibid., pp. 54-55.
131. Ibid., pp. 77-78.
132. *Mail and Empire*, 14 Dec. 1907, 20.
133. Ibid., 27 Oct. 1906, 20.
134. Rosen, Chap. 8.
135. *Mail and Empire*, 21 Mar. 1908, 13.
136. "The Genuine Aim of Suffragettes," Ibid., 19 Sept. 1908, 14.
137. Ibid., 9 May 1908, 20.
138. Ibid., 20 June 1908, 20.
139. Cleverdon, pp. 30-31.
140. Ibid., pp. 11, 36.
141. See, for example, the Hamilton *Herald*, 5 June 1911, 2.
142. PAC Media Club of Canada, Vol. 1. 1909-1910 Annual Report. The club had voted to affiliate with the National Council the year before but the move was delayed due to an oversight by the press club's reporting secretary. Ibid., 1907-1908 Annual Report, 10.
143. *Mail and Empire*, 19 June 1909, 20.
144. Ibid., 18 June 1909, pp. 1, 5.
145. Ibid., 22 June 1909, pp. 1, 11.
146. Ibid., 21 June 1909, pp. 1, 5.
147. Ibid., 25 June 1909, pp. 1, 10.
148. Ibid., 23 June 1909, 6. More progressive newspapers strongly endorsed suffrage. See, for example, the Toronto *World*, 23 Oct. 1909, 1. Lady Aberdeen's declaration and the ICW's support legitimized the suffrage position, although most Canadians still had

limited awareness of—or interest in—the issue. Strong-Boag, *Parliament of Women*, pp. 275-276.

149. *Mail and Empire*, 7 Aug. 1909, 16.
150. Ibid., 25 Sept. 1909, 21.
151. Ibid., 9 Oct. 1909, 20; Ibid., 20 Nov. 1909, 20.
152. Cleverdon, pp. 16-17.
153. *Mail and Empire*, 20 Nov. 1909, 21.
154. Rosen, pp. 93; 177-178.
155. *Mail and Empire*, 20 Nov. 1909, 18. Rosen also accuses the Pankhursts of autocracy. Rosen, Ch. 14.
156. *Mail and Empire*, 22 Nov. 1909, pp. 1, 4. "The Flaneur" ignored Mrs. Pankhurst's visit altogether. Ibid., 27 Nov. 1909, 17.
157. Ibid., 20.
158. *Mail and Empire*, 22 Nov. 1909, 20.
159. Ibid., 15 Jan. 1910, 20. Kit hoped Canadian women would not use the same tactics. Ibid., 15 Jan. 1910, 20. Newspaper editors also condemned the violence. The Hamilton *Herald* described the Suffragette movement as "dementia" in an "epidemic" form and said its adherents should not be treated as criminals but as mental patients. Hamilton *Herald*, 16 Aug. 1913, 6.
160. Response to "Outsider," *Mail and Empire*, 19 March 1910, 21. Her endorsement preceded that of the National Council of Women by four months. Cleverdon, pp. 164-165.
161. *Mail and Empire*, 26 Mar. 1910, 20.
162. A colleague, Jean Graham, wrote that "Kit ...surrendered like myself to the charm of Mrs. Pankhurst." See "At Five O'Clock," *Canadian Magazine* 34 (Dec. 1909-Apr. 1910), pp. 286-289.
163. *Mail and Empire*, 2 Apr. 1910, 21.
164. Speaking in general terms, she later admitted: "I never craved the office of neuter worker bee....The role of Queen Bee seems to me the most preferable." Hamilton *Herald*, 28 Sept. 1912, 7.
165. According to Schudson, this trend did not really take hold until after the First World War, although he notes that other experts would argue it started with the establishment of the wire services before the turn of the century. Schudson, pp. 3-6.
166. Hamilton *Herald*, 12 Aug. 1911, 5. See also another response to "Suffragette," Ibid., 2 Nov. 1912, 7.
167. The Flora Macdonald Denison column is in the Thomas Fisher Rare Book Library, the University of Toronto, F.M. Denison MS. Collection 51, Box 8A, File marked 1911-1913, copy of "The Open Road Toward Democracy," in the Toronto *Sunday World*, n.d., n.p.
168. Vancouver *News Advertiser*, 16 Nov. 1913, 10.
169. Ibid.

170. *Mail and Empire*, 3 July 1909, 20. See also Ibid., 1 Jan. 1909, 17 and 1 Jan. 1910, 20. A few years later, she explained that a cheery philosophy had been fashionable in women's pages at the time, and she had since come to believe that suffering should not be denied or hidden. Hamilton *Herald*, 9 Aug. 1913, 23.
171. *Mail and Empire*, 5 Nov. 1910, 23.
172. Ibid., 3 Dec. 1910, 23; letters from "Jack and Jill" in "Kit's Comments," Ibid., 15 Dec. 1910, 15 and from "One of a Hundred" and "Betty Blue" in "Woman's Kingdom," Ibid., 24 Dec. 1910, 15.
173. "Kit's Corner," Ibid., 7 Nov. 1910, 13.
174. "Woman's Kingdom," 7 Jan. 1911, 20.
175. "Kit" to Katherine Hale, op. cit.
176. *Mail and Empire*, 11 Feb. 1911, pp. 20-21. Her last signed "Women's Kingdom" had appeared 4 Feb. 1911, 20, with no farewell in evidence.
177. Response to "A Shadow (Toronto)," Hamilton *Herald*, 1 July 1911, 3.
178. Response to "Puzzled," Ibid., 24 June 1911, 7.
179. Correspondence in PAC K.B.C. Papers, Vol. 4, File 4.
180. Response to "Old Reader," Hamilton *Herald*, 26 Aug. 1911, 7. She found female editors to be much more helpful and easier to deal with than the males. Ibid., 1 July 1911, 3.
181. The Stratford *Daily Beacon*, 6 Jan. 1912, 9. She apparently charged each newspaper five dollars per column. Ferguson, 9.
182. "The Pedlar's Pack," *Canada Monthly*, February 1911, pp. 303-308.
183. After 29 June 1912 the *Beacon* dropped "Kit's Column" altogether, with no explanation.
184. Hamilton *Herald*, 5 Aug. 1911, 7.
185. Her parentheses. Stratford *Daily Beacon*, 13 Jan. 1912, 11.
186. Response to "Mere Man," Ibid., 20 Jan. 1912, 11.
187. Ibid., 15 June 1912, 10. She did believe in an afterlife. Hamilton *Herald*, 27 July 1912, 7.
188. *Canada Monthly*, Sept. 1914, 346 and Ibid., January 1915, 182.
189. Gartshore-Waterous Interview.
190. Hamilton *Herald*, 23 Aug. 1913, 7; *Canada Monthly*, September 1913, 44.
191. Response to "An Autumn Leaf," *Mail and Empire*, 9 Oct. 1909, 21.
192. Her husband was John Gartshore, an Ancaster, Ontario farmer. See his obituary, PAC K.B.C. Papers, Vol. 4, File 4 undated newspaper clipping. See also Kit's poem, "The Parting," addressed to "my one ewe-lamb," about the separation of a mother and her daughter. Vancouver *News Advertiser*, 20 Apr. 1913, 31.
193. Her granddaughter Kit Waterous comments: "Well, the world *was* coming to an end, as she had known it." Gartshore-Waterous

Interview. Kit was not alone in her beliefs. In Britain, the Suffragette leader Christabel Pankhurst devoted her life after the war to preaching about the imminent second coming of Christ. Rosen, 270.

194. Hamilton *Herald*, 19 Sept. 1914, 8. When a reader asked her to eschew war and write about something happy, she indicated that her editor wanted "war stuff" but obliged with a feature on Indian summer. *Canada Monthly*, Nov. 1914, 40.

195. Hamilton *Herald*, 26 Sept. 1914, 8. She did not believe, however, that if women ran the world, there would be no more war. "Oh, wouldn't there be? The Pedlar in his long life tramps knows a thing or two..." *Canada Monthly*, March 1915, 344.

196. She complained that the demand for war copy was costing many women journalists their newspaper columns. Hamilton *Herald*, 5 Sept. 1914, 8.

197. Ibid., 3 Oct. 1914, 8.

198. Doctor Coleman was terribly upset that he had been unable to save his wife. After she died, he joined the armed forces and served overseas during the war. He later remarried. Gartshore-Waterous Interview.

199. He died within a year of his mother. Ibid.

200. Like her mother, Patsy was also to lose a child. Within a year of her mother's and brother's deaths, her son Bill accidently drowned at the age of two. She had another son and a daughter—J.B. Gartshore and Kit Waterous. Her brother had never married. Ibid.

201. *Canada Monthly*, June 1915, pp. 102-104. The original manuscript is in PAC K.B.C. Papers, Vol. 2, File 4.

CONCLUSION

I decided to examine the life and work of Kathleen Blake Coleman because the history of Canadian women journalists in Canada has only begun to be explored and my own, predominantly female, journalism students don't know who their foremothers are. Most have never heard of Coleman—or Agnes Maule Machar, Sara Jeannette Duncan, Alice Fenton Freeman and the other journalists I have mentioned. I chose to examine Kit, not just because of her prominence, but because there was something about the vividness and warmth of her journalism that appealed to me as much as it did many of her own generation.

I hoped to write a biographical account of a feminist heroine, but there were, I quickly discovered, two problems with that. First of all, Kit would not have called herself a feminist and second, Kathleen did not leave behind enough evidence about herself to permit that kind of examination. Instead, I have taken into consideration what feminist scholars have written about women writers and how their public voices have been constrained. The result is a study of "Kit," a puzzling and fascinating public persona, a woman journalist who logically would have been expected to embrace the major goals of the feminist movement of her day, but didn't.

In examining the lives and work of women journalists, it is important to look at the constraints placed upon them in the profession. To do anything less is to risk distortion. As Rutherford has pointed out, what was important in

165

nineteenth century journalism was that certain "truths" be promulgated. The writer of the women's page was expected to stress what were considered acceptable standards of thought and behaviour for women.

Kit was torn, in her desire for success, between what was an acceptable writing style for a female—sentiment and "gossip"—and what was becoming the male model of journalism—linear, objective, rational discourse on the political and economic events of the day. Her sense of editorial freedom and accomplishment lay in how often she could write about intelligent topics. The fact that she had to fight for even those privileges was an indication that the editors of her day barely acknowledged the intelligence of their female readers. Even her most ambitious undertaking—her assignment as a war correspondent in Cuba—was limited by the assumption that she was writing from a woman's point of view.

When one considers that Kathleen's economic survival and that of her children depended, for much of her career, on how she projected Kit's personality, it is not surprising to find inconsistency in her treatment of issues vital to women in general and confusion, anxiety and antagonism towards women activists in particular. It is true that she demonstrated real courage when it came to questions that touched on her own experiences—such as economic hardship—but she was also very afraid, it seems, of appearing "masculine" by supporting other planks in the feminist platform. In her mind, equal pay for equal work was only just if you were, as she was, a woman solely responsible for the financial support of your children. But she was perhaps too timid on other matters, such as suffrage and the equality of the sexes in marriage, because of a need for economic security, and public and professional approbation of her as a woman writer.

What she wrote of her background would suggest that she remained especially afraid of becoming destitute, the way she had been as a widow and immigrant, suffering "poverty and hunger, absolute, primitive hunger when the steaming odor of savory soups from restaurants used to turn me faint and sick."[1] That was true even after she married Doctor Coleman. She wrote that she became a journalist in order to earn a living and not out of any feminist desire for self-fulfillment:

> I have never advocated what is called "New-womanism." I became a journalist through the necessity that calls for bread for the children. I have little sympathy for your fashionable Madam, for my heart lies close to that of the working woman, the woman who has the harder task. There are many gentlewomen working today—women highly-educated, sensitive, hyper-sensitive because of that very education, because of the luxurious surroundings of early life.[2]

At the same time, one must remember that, despite her protestations, economic security was not her only reason for staying in the profession. She admitted that she loved journalism for itself, "not so much for the salary as for the love of the game, for the endeavour, the fight, the win!"[3]

There were a lot of contradictions in what she wrote, contradictions that were a reflection of the changing role of women in the nineteenth century. She was certainly no different from many of them in her elation over the greater opportunities presented by broader education and new openings in the work place, opportunities that also bred confusion over proper gender roles and fear of not belonging. Historian Carol Dyhouse put it well when she wrote of Victorian women who, like Kit, were brought up to be "unselfish" and to put home duties first, but found themselves in other roles:

> A total rejection of the understanding about femininity and the patterns of relationship between men and women learned in the family was probably comparatively rare. It was much more common to find mature women who were still in some way troubled about their self-image, their femininity: consciously or unconsciously ambivalent about their feminine role. Women who stepped aside from convention and carved out careers for themselves outside the home—particularly those who became feminists—illustrate these conflicts in their attitudes and personalities, sometimes in an acute form.

167

Such women often entered professions which allowed them to adopt a "mothering" role; it helped assuage the guilt they felt at not being self-sacrificing enough.[4]

Kathleen did not ignore the maternal aspect of Kit, even at the beginning; in fact, it was one of the main reasons for her appeal. Her maternity was her shield, especially after she introduced her children into the "Kingdom." Motherhood was powerful in her time, more powerful than claims to a sense of adventure or equal intellect with men. But she also insisted that the assumed male attributes of intelligence, adventuresomeness and ambition belonged to women, too. Those characteristics also played a great role in her public persona, as risky as her androgynous manifestations of them sometimes were for a "proper" lady. That they worked for her is apparent in an unsigned obituary published after her death in the Toronto *Globe*: "Kit had abundantly the mother-mind and the mother-nature, their outpouring being through channels of gaiety and tears, and an intellectuality masculine in range and definiteness."[5]

But this dichotomy also resulted in contradictions that can be seen in many of the columns she produced during her twenty-five years in journalism. The Irish hunter swears man-like at her horse while claiming status as a Victorian gentlewoman. She believes women are equally as intelligent as men but are not knowledgeable enough to vote. She declares herself in favour of equal pay for equal work but accepts on authority the denigrating remarks a male boss makes about his female workers. A woman can travel widely and adventure freely but her real happiness almost always hinges on marriage and motherhood.

That Kit felt these contradictions keenly herself is apparent in her struggles to escape her domestic sphere through travel and, at the same time, come to terms with the conflict between the need to create and the necessity of earning a living. She finally acquiesced to more limited horizons than she had first imagined, partly because she also craved emotional security. Her depressions—and perhaps her illnesses, too—were a side-effect of her attempts to balance her different needs.

How much can one believe of what she wrote? There is no easy answer. Literary licence in newspaper writing was quite acceptable in the nineteenth century—some might argue that it still is—but its purpose was what counted: to educate and entertain. The "Kingdom" had its own formula for people-pleasing. Kit's obvious lapses into fabrication should be seen in that light and in that of the deadline demands of the newspaper profession, not as any cynical attempt to mislead or betray. As she once wrote, revealingly, to a reader who was apparently puzzled by her contradictory comments:

> J.A.R.S. (Hamilton).—It is easy enough to "put a dog", as you put it, in one's writing, and it is very commonly done. But it is foolish, I think. For instance, not long ago someone said to me that they thought one was "very hard up"—on the edge of starvation in fact—through little things one wrote now and again about home life and that sort of thing. Perhaps I consider riches to be more of a matter of millions— hundreds of thousands—than mere little thousands and hundreds. But that is a very different matter from being really poor, you know... The trouble with scribes like myself is that some people take everything one says quite literally... Someone writes "You seem for (the suffragettes) one day and against them the next." Lor', man, one must write something—oh, well—let it go at that.[6]

Kit was an enigma in more ways than one. Despite her "closeness" to her "paper-children" readers, she was a distant figure. With just about every private and public domestic issue she touched upon, she played the expert/mother role but rarely became involved herself. Although her writing would indicate that she cared passionately about the poor and downtrodden, especially children, she did not become a social reform crusader. She rarely offered her personal, as opposed to her professional, help to her readers, but kept her distance as journalists usually do. In reality, she would not, with her work schedule, have had the time to become involved and, because she was essentially a loner, did not want to do so.

She was a woman apart, also, in that not many Canadian women came from the same kind of privileged background, were as well read, or travelled and wrote the way she did. But that was appealing; it made her a romantic figure, and one who could inspire young women journalists. That is the way she liked it; or, as she herself noted, she would rather be the queen bee than the drone.[7]

Because she had very few close women friends—Jean Blewett being the exception—even female colleagues who were her contemporaries knew her only from afar. To them, she was a brave pioneer because, more than anything, she tried to broaden what used to be considered women's sphere, or, as a contemporary explained, she had: "..a glorious vision of a woman's kingdom not always cluttered by cook-books and fashion-plates but wide and wonderful as the world itself."[8]

In her own world of journalism, Kit was an outsider in what was still a man's profession. Her impatience over that state of affairs finally prompted her to do something that was really quite uncharacteristic of her—she got involved in a woman's organization. Although her role in the Canadian Women's Press Club was limited, and its own professional stance cautious, she did help get it started. Her personal shyness and the fact that her health had begun to fail probably limited her involvement as much as her "loner" tendencies, but she could also be very kind and helpful, especially to the "cubs," as many of them have testified.

Her experiences with the press club was important in that it allowed her to work with activist women, a turn of events that led to her acceptance of the women's movement and, eventually, suffrage—but only after a great deal of ambivalence. In the context of late nineteenth century Canada, Kit was neither as conservative nor as liberal as she has been made out to be. She held what we today would probably call a "middle of the road" position, which is exactly what the standards of conventional journalism demand.

What remained outstanding about her was her tolerance, particularly in regard to people of different religions and nations (although, as was typical of her time, not often of different races). Her antipathy toward war did not begin in Cuba, but many years before in Ireland, where she witnessed sectarian violence. Although she paid lip service to British power of Empire, she was very critical of jingoism, particularly of the kind demonstrated by newspapers. Her essential humanism was amply demonstrated during both the Spanish-American and the First World Wars.

The mystery of her real identity still remains. "Kit" was a woman who struggled as a journalist but wanted literary success, who became depressed when her dreams began to fade, and who finally was content to earn her living as a women's page columnist, do some travelling and have a happy home besides. That she earned some fame and recognition was a bonus, one not granted to many women who wrote.

She may have been very like the real Kathleen Blake Coleman, whoever she was, or quite different. The few letters that survived Kathleen's death, her grandchildren's stories, Kit's accounts of her home-life and the biographical sketches written by her contemporaries suggest that the persona and the woman were very similar, especially as she became established as a journalist. There was much in her writing that would suggest that many times, she was trying to communicate with her readers about her own life, but was not sure she should do so. Passionate bursts of thinly veiled confidences alternating with reserved declarations of her right to privacy were typical and suggest a woman who wanted to say who she really was but was often afraid.

And so, she remained an enigma, even almost twenty years after her death, as an unsigned clipping from the Hamilton *Herald* attests:

> Kit was one of those rare people about whom legends had
> arisen even during her own life-time. Strangeness, beauty
> and apartness were the qualities in any one about whom leg-
> ends flowed. Singularly close to her large public, Kit was yet
> private and withdrawn. She hated publicity as to her own
> affairs. She understood people but did not expect people to
> understand her. She had been possessed of that "artistic sen-
> sitiveness" which made all great artists a strange, lonely race.[9]

Essentially, Kathleen/Kit created herself. By exploiting the
contradictory aspects of her own nature and, thereby, keeping herself a mystery, she took her identity into her own
hands, giving herself a source of personal power in a time
when women had very little.

Notes

1. Response to "Governess," *Mail and Empire*, 12 Aug. 1905, 19.
2. Ibid., 22 Nov. 1902, 18.
3. Ibid., 3 Apr. 1909, 20.
4. Carol Dyhouse, *Girls Growing Up in Late Victorian and Edwardian England* (London: Routledge and Kegan Paul 1981), pp. 34-36.
5. Undated clipping in PAC K.B.C. Papers, Vol. 2, File 30.
6. Stratford *Daily Beacon*, 27 April 1912, 12.
7. Hamilton *Herald*, 28 Sept. 1912, 7. op. cit.
8. Burkholder, pp. 6-7.
9. PAC K.B.C. Papers, Vol. 2, File 35, "Women Honour Kit's Memory," Hamilton *Spectator*, 18 April 1934, 2.

BIBLIOGRAPHY

Abel, Elizabeth (ed.) *Writing and Sexual Difference*. Chicago: The University of Chicago Press 1982.

Acton, J., P. Goldsmith and B. Shepard (eds.) *Women at Work, Ontario 1850-1930*. Toronto: Canadian Women's Educational Press 1974.

Adams, Catherine. "Sara Jeannette Duncan's Contributions to The Week." Unpublished M.A. thesis, Institute of Canadian Studies, Carleton University 1980.

Allan, Richard. *The Social Passion: Religion and Social Reform in Canada 1914-1928*. Toronto: University of Toronto Press 1971.

Ascher, Carol, Louise A. Di Salvo and Sara Reddick (eds.) *Between Women*. Boston: Beacon Press 1984.

Austin, Rev. B.F. (ed.) *Woman: Her Character, Culture and Calling*. Brantford, Ont: Book and Bible House 1890.

Avery, Heather. "One Author's Response to a Changing World: A Study of the Variations in Selected Novels of Lucy Maud Montgomery." Unpublished M.A. thesis, Carleton University 1985.

Bacchi, Carol Lee. *Liberation Deferred? The Ideas of the English-Canadian Suffragists, 1877-1918*. Toronto: University of Toronto Press 1983.

Bannerman, Jean. *Leading Ladies, Canada 1639-1967*. Galt, Ont: Highland Press, 1967 rev. Dundas Ont. Carrswood 1977.

175

Barber, Marilyn. "Below Stairs: The Domestic Servant." In *Material History Bulletin*, 19, Ottawa, Spring 1984. National Museum of Man.

――――. "The Women Ontario Welcomed: Immigrant Domestics for Ontario Homes, 1870-1930." In Alison Prentice and Susan Mann Trofimenkoff (eds.) *The Neglected Majority*, Vol. II. Toronto: McClelland and Stewart 1985.

Bennett, E.A. *Journalism for Women*. London: John Lane 1898.

Berger, Carl and Ramsay Cook (eds.) *The West and the Nation* Toronto: McClelland and Stewart 1976.

Blewett, Jean. *Jean Blewett's Poems*. Toronto: McClelland and Stewart 1922.

Blore, Betty. "Women's Liberation as Portrayed in the Writings of Nellie McClung and Francis Marion Beynon: An Agrarian Reform Perspective." Unpublished M.A. research essay, Institute of Canadian Studies, Carleton University 1982.

Bouvin, Aurelien et Kenneth Landry. "Francoise et Madeleine: pionnieres du journalisme feminin au Quebec." In *Atlantis*, Vol. 4, N. 1. Automne 1978.

Brouwer, Ruth Compton. "The Between-Age Christianity of Agnes Maule Machar." In *Canadian Historical Review*, Vol. LXV, No. 3, Sept. 1984.

Brown, Charles H. *The Correspondents' War*. New York: Charles Scribner's Sons 1967.

――――. "A Woman's Odyssey: The War Correspondence of Anna Benjamin." In *Journalism Quarterly*, Autumn 1969.

Brown, Robert Craig and Ramsay Cook. *Canada 1896-1921—A Nation Transformed*. Toronto: McClelland and Stewart 1974.

Bunce-Jones, Mark. *Twilight of the Ascendancy*. London: Constable 1987.

Burkholder, Mabel. *"Kit": Pioneer Canadian Newspaperwoman.* Hamilton Women's Press Club 1933.

Cameron, Agnes Deans. *The New North.* New York: D. Appleton and Co. 1910.

Canadian Press Association. *A History of Canadian Journalism.* Toronto: Canadian Press Association 1908, rev. 1958.

Caudill, Ed. "A Content Analysis of Press Views of Darwin's Evolution Theory, 1860-1925." In *Journalism Quarterly,* Winter 1987.

Charlesworth, Hector. *Candid Chronicles.* Toronto: MacMillan of Canada 1925.

Chenier, Nancy. "Agnes Maule Machar: Her Life, Her Social Concerns and a Preliminary Biography of Her Writing." Unpublished M.A. thesis, Institute of Canadian Studies, Carleton University 1977.

Clark, C.S. *Of Toronto the Good: The Queen City of Canada As It Is.* Toronto: Toronto Publishing Company 1898, repr. Coles Publishing 1970.

Cleverdon, Catherine L. *The Woman Suffrage Movement in Canada.* Intro. Ramsay Cook. Toronto: University of Toronto Press 1974, repr. 1978.

Clio Collective. *Quebec Women—A History,* Trans. Roger Gannon and Rosalind Gill. Toronto: The Women's Press 1987.

Coburn, Judi. "'I See and Am Silent', A Short History of Nursing in Ontario." In J. Acton et al. (eds.), *Women at Work.*

Cook, Ramsay. *The Politics of John W. Dafoe and the Free Press.* Toronto: University of Toronto Press 1963.

————. *The Regenerators-Social Criticism in Late Victorian English Canada.* Toronto: University of Toronto Press 1985.

————. 'Francis Marion Beynon and the Crisis in Christian Reformism." In Carl Berger and Ramsay Cook (eds.) *The West and the Nation.*

——— and Wendy Mitchinson (eds.) *The Proper Sphere— Woman's Place in Canadian Society*. Toronto: Oxford University Press 1976.

Covert, Cathy L. "Journalism History and Women's Experience: A Problem in Conceptual Change." In *Journalism History* 8:1, Spring 1981.

Cranston, Herbert. *Ink On My Fingers*. Toronto: Ryerson Press 1953.

Cumming, Carman. "The Toronto *Daily Mail*, Edward Farrer and the Question of Canadian-American Union." *Journal of Canadian Studies*, Spring 1989.

Cunningham, Gail. *The New Woman and the Victorian Novel*. London: MacMillan 1978.

Daly, Mary. *Gyn/Ecology*. Boston: Beacon Press 1978.

Denison, Grace E. *A Happy Holiday*. Toronto: Grace E. Denison 1890.

Dickens, Charles. *Oliver Twist*. Intro. Humphrey House. Toronto: Oxford University Press 1970.

Duncan, Sara Jeannette. *A Social Departure: How Orthodocia and I Went Around the World by Ourselves*. New York: Appleton 1890.

———. *A Daughter of Today*. Intro. Misao Dean. Ottawa: The Tecumseh Press 1988.

———. *Cousin Cinderella: A Canadian Girl in London*. Toronto: MacMillan and Co. 1908.

Dyhouse, Carol. *Girls Growing Up in Late Victorian and Edwardian England*. London: Routledge, Kegan Paul 1981.

Faderman, Lillian. *Surpassing the Love of Men: Romantic Friendship and Love Between Women from the Renaissance to the Present*. New York: William Morrow and Company 1981.

Ferguson, Ted. *Kit Coleman, Queen of Hearts*. Toronto: Doubleday 1978.

Fitz-patrick, W.J. *The Life of the Very Reverend Thomas N. Burke.* London: Kegan Paul, Trench and Co., 1885.

Flexner, Eleanor. *Century of Struggle-the Woman's Rights Movement in the United States.* New York: Atheneum 1970.

Foner, Philip S. *The Spanish-Cuban-American War and the Birth of American Imperialism 1895-1902,* Vols. I and II. New York and London: Monthly Review Press 1972.

Foster, Jeannette. *Sex Variant Women in Literature.* Vantage Press 1956 repr. Naiad Press Inc. 1985.

Foster, Shirley. *Victorian Women's Fiction: Marriage, Freedom and the Individual.* London: Croom Helm 1985.

Freeman, Barbara M. "'An Impertinent Fly': Canadian Journalist Kathleen Blake Watkins Covers the Spanish-American War." In *Journalism History,* 15:4, Summer 1989.

————. "'Every Stroke Upward': Women Journalists in Canada 1880-1906." In *Canadian Women's Studies,* Vol. 7, No. 3, Fall 1986. Reprinted in Laurence Steven, Douglas Parker and Jack Lewis (eds.) *From Reading to Writing: A Reader, Rhetoric and Handbook.* Toronto: Prentice-Hall Canada 1988.

Geller, Gloria. "The Wartime Elections Act of 1917 and the Canadian Women's Movement." In *Atlantis* Vol. 2, No. 1. Fall 1976.

Goddard, Barbara. "A Portrait With Three Faces: The New Woman in Fiction by Canadian Women 1880-1920." In *The Literary Criterion,* Vol. 19, Nos. 3 & 4, 1984.

Goodwin, Rae E. "The Early Journalism of Sara Jeannette Duncan." Unpublished M.A. thesis, University of Toronto 1964.

Gordon, Linda. *Woman's Body, Woman's Right—A Social History of Birth Control in America.* New York: Penguin Books 1977.

Gorham, Deborah. *The Victorian Girl and the Feminine Ideal.* Indiana University Press 1982.

———. "English Militancy and the Canadian Suffrage Movement." In *Atlantis*, Vol. 1, No. 1, Fall 1975.

———. "The Canadian Suffragists." In Gwen Matheson (ed.) *Women in the Canadian Mosaic.* Toronto: Peter Martin 1976.

———. "Pen and Buckskin: Women Journalists in the West Who Knew Wheat and Justice." In *Content* May 1978.

———. "Flora MacDonald Denison: Canadian Feminist." In L. Kealey (ed.) *A Not Unreasonable Claim.*

Green, Constance McLaughlin. *The Church On Lafayette Square 1815-1970.* Washington: Potomac Boos Inc. 1970.

Gwyn, Sandra. *The Private Capital.* Toronto: McClelland and Stewart 1984.

Hacker, Carlotta. *The Indominable Lady Doctors.* Halifax, N.S: Formac Publishing—Goodread Biographies 1984.

Haig, Kennethe M. *Brave Harvest: The Life Story of E. Cora Hind.* Toronto: Thomas Allen 1945.

Ham, George. *Reminiscences of a Raconteur.* Toronto: Musson 1925.

Harkness, Ross. *J.E. Atkinson of the Star.* Toronto: University of Toronto Press 1963.

Henry, Susan J. "Private Lives: An Added Dimension for Understanding Journalism History." In *Journalism History*, 6:4. Winter 1979-1980.

———. "Changing Media History Through Women's History." In Pamela J. Creddon (ed.) *Women in Mass Communications—Challenging Gender Values.* Sage Publications-Focus Editions, Vol. 106, Summer 1989.

Houston, Susan E. "Victorian Origins of Juvenile Delinquency." In *History of Education Quarterly*, Vol. XII, June 1972.

———. "Waifs and Strays of a Late Victorian City: Juvenile Delinquents in Toronto." In Joy Parr (ed.) *The Family in Canadian History.* Toronto: McClelland and Stewart 1982.

Jones, Andrew and Leo Rutman. *In the Children's Aid: J.J. Kelso and Child Welfare in Ontario.* Toronto: University of Toronto Press 1981.

Kealey, Linda (ed.), *A Not Unreasonable Claim: Women and Reform in Canada 1880s-1920s.* Toronto: Canadian Women's Educational Press 1979.

Kealey, Wayne. *Working Class Toronto at the Turn of the Century.* Toronto: New Hogtown Press 1973.

Kelso, J.J. *Early History of the Humane and Children's Aid Movement in Ontario 1886-1893.* Toronto: King's Publisher, L.K. Cameron 1911.

Kesterton, W.H. *The History of Journalism in Canada.* Toronto: MacMillan of Canada. Carleton University Library Series No. 36. 1978.

Kinsman, Gary. *The Regulation of Desire—Sexuality in Canada.* Montreal: Black Rose Books 1987.

Kit. *To London for the Jubilee.* Toronto: Morang 1897.

Klein, Alice and Wayne Roberts. "Besieged Innocence: The 'Problem' and Problems of Working Women—Toronto, 1896-1914." In J. Acton et al. (eds.) *Women at Work.*

Knightley, Philip. *The First Casualty.* New York and London: Harcourt Brace Jovanovich 1975.

Kroller, Eve-Marie. *The Canadian Traveller in Europe 1851-1900.* Vancouver: University of British Columbia Press 1987.

Lacelle, Claudette. "Les domestiques dans les villes canadiennes aux XIXe siecle: effectifs et conditions de vie." En *Histoire sociale*, Vol. XV, N. 29.

Lang, Marjory. "Separate Entrances: The First Generation of Canadian Women Journalists." In Lorraine McMullen (ed.) *Re(Dis)covering Our Foremothers: Nineteenth Century Canadian Women Writers.* Ottawa: University of Ottawa Press 1989.

Lapsley, Jane Turner. "Sara Jeannette Duncan and Archibald Lampman: Two Social Critics of the Idea of

Progress in Victorian Canada." Unpublished Masters research essay, Institute of Canadian Studies, Carleton University 1985.

Lee, Joseph. "Women and the Church since the Famine." In Margaret MacCurtain and Donncha O Corrain (eds.), *Women in Irish History*. Dublin: Arlen House, The Women's Press 1978.

Leslie, Genevieve. "Domestic Service in Canada, 1880-1920." In J. Acton et al (eds.) *Women at Work*.

Lewis, Jane. "Women Lost and Found—The Impact of Feminism on History." In Dale Spender (ed.) *Men's Studies Modified*.

Light, Beth and Joy Parr (eds.) *Canadian Women on the Move 1867-1920*. Toronto: New Hogtown Press/OISE 1983.

MacAree, J.V. *The Fourth Column*. Toronto: Macmillan of Canada 1934.

MacCurtain, Margaret. "Women, the Vote and Revolution." In Margaret MacCurtain and Donncha O Corrain (eds.) *Women in Irish History*.

Machar, Agnes Maule. *Roland Graeme, Knight*. Toronto: W. Briggs 1906.

MacLaren Angus and Arlene Tigar. *The Bedroom and the State*. Toronto: McClelland and Stewart 1986.

MacBeth, Madge. *Boulevard Career*. Toronto: Kingswood House 1957.

Macdonald N. and A. Chaiton (eds.) *Egerton Ryerson and His Times*. Toronto: MacMillan and Co. 1978.

MacGill, E. G. *My Mother the Judge*. Toronto: Ryerson Press 1955.

Matheson, Gwen (ed.) *Women in the Canadian Mosaic*. Toronto: Peter Martin 1976.

Marzolf, Marion. *Up from the Footnote*. New York: Hastings House 1978.

McGlashan, Zena Beth. "Women Witness the Russian Revolution: Analyzing Ways of Seeing." In *Journalism History*, 12:2 Summer 1985.

Mitchinson, Wendy. "The WCTU: 'For God, Home and Native Land': A Study in Nineteenth-Century Feminism." In Linda Kealey (ed.) *A Not Unreasonable Claim*.

Moers, Ellen. *Literary Women*. New York: Doubleday and Company 1976.

Montgomery, L.M. *The Alpine Path: The Story of My Career*. 1917 repr. Toronto: Fitzhenry and Whiteside 1976.

Moodie, Susanna. *Roughing It in the Bush*. Intro. Carl F. Klinck. Toronto: McClelland and Stewart, 1983.

Morgan, Henry. *Men and Women of the Time*. Toronto: W. Briggs 1912.

———. *Types of Canadian Women*. Toronto: W. Briggs 1903.

Morrison, W.R. "Their Proper Sphere: Feminism, the Family and Child-Centred Social Reform in Ontario, 1885-1900." In *Ontario History*, Vol. LXVIII, Nos. 1 and 2, Mar. and June 1976.

National Council of Women of Canada. *Women Workers of Canada*. Ottawa: National Council of Women of Canada 1898.

———. *Women of Canada and Their Work* 1900. Ottawa: National Council of Women of Canada repr. 1975.

Normand, Edward. *A History of Ireland*. London: Allan Lane— The Penguin Press 1971.

Olasky, Marvin. *The Press and Abortion 1838 - 1988*. New Jersey: Laurence Erlbaum Associates 1988.

———. "Hawks or Doves: Texas Press and Spanish-American War." In *Journalism Quarterly*, Vol. 64, No. 1. Spring 1987.

Olsen, Tillie. *Silences*. New York: Laurel Edition, Dell Publishing Co. Inc. 1983.

O'Toole, G.J.A. *The Spanish War—An American Epic-1898.* New York and London: W.W. Norton and Company 1984.

Palmer, Howard, (ed.) *Immigration and the Rise of Multiculturalism.* Toronto: Copp Clark 1975.

Parr, Joy. (ed.) *The Family in Canadian History.* Toronto: McClelland and Stewart 1982.

————. *Labouring Children: British Immigrant Apprentices to Canada 1869-1924.* Montreal: McGill-Queen's University Press 1980.

————. "Transplanting from Dens of Iniquity: Theology and Child Migration." In L. Kealey (ed.) *A Not Unreasonable Claim.*

Prentice, Alison. *The School Promoters: Education and Social Class in Mid-Nineteenth Century Upper Canada.* Toronto: McClelland and Stewart 1977.

———— and Susan Houston (eds.) *Family, School and Society in 19th Century Canada.* Toronto: Oxford University Press 1975.

———— and Susan Mann Trofimenkoff (eds.) *The Neglected Majority,* Vols. I and II. Toronto: McClelland and Stewart 1977, 1985.

————. "The Feminization of Teaching." In Alison Prentice and Susan Mann Trofimenkoff (eds.) *The Neglected Majority,* Vol. 1.

Ridley, Amy. "'The Dual Struggle': Mary-Agnes FitzGibbon, Toronto Journalist 1899-1907." Unpublished Masters research essay, Institute of Canadian Studies, Carleton University 1983.

Roberts, Barbara. "'Why Do Women Do Nothing to End the War?': Canadian Feminists-Pacifists and the Great War." Ottawa: Canadian Research Institute for the Advancement of Women—1985. The CRIAW Papers, No. 13.

————. "'A Work of Empire': Canadian Reformers and British Female Immigration." In L. Kealey (ed.) *A Not Unreasonable Claim.*

Roberts, Wayne. *Honest Womanhood: Feminism, Femininity and Class Consciousness Among Toronto Working Women, 1896-1914.* Toronto: New Hogtown Press 1977.

————. "Rocking the Cradle for the World, the New Woman and Maternal Feminism, Toronto, 1877-1914." In L. Kealey (ed.) *A Not Unreasonable Claim.*

Rochford, J.A. (ed.) *Father Burke's Sermons and Lectures.* New York: P.J. Kennedy, Excelsior Catholic Publishing House 1905.

Rosen, Andrew. *Rise Up Women! The Militant Campaign of the Women's Social and Political Union 1903-1914.* London and Boston: Routledge and Kegan Paul 1974.

Ross, Ishbel. *Ladies of the Press; the story of women in journalism by an insider.* New York and London: Harper 1936.

Ross, P.D. *Retrospects of A Newspaper Person.* Toronto: Oxford University Press 1931.

Rotenberg, Lori. "The Wayward Worker, Toronto's Prostitute at the Turn of the Century." In J.Acton et al. (eds.) *Women at Work.*

Rowland Robin. "Kit Watkins: World's First Accredited Woman War Correspondent." In *Content,* May 1978 repr. in B. Zwicker and D. MacDonald (eds.) *The News: Inside the Canadian Media.* Ottawa: Deneau Publishers 1982.

————. "Kit's Secret." In *Content,* November 1978.

Rubio, Mary and Elizabeth Waterson, (eds.) *The Selected Journals of Lucy Maude Montgomery.* Vol. I: 1889-1910. Toronto: Oxford University Press 1985.

Russ, Joanna. *How To Suppress Women's Writing.* Austin: University of Texas 1983.

Rutherford, Paul. *A Victorian Authority—The Daily Press in Late Nineteenth Century Canada.* Toronto: University of Toronto Press 1982.

————. *The Making of the Canadian Media*. Toronto McGraw-Hill Ryerson 1978.

Saunders, Marshall. *Beautiful Joe*. Philadelphia: Charles Banes-Holiday Edition 1893; repr. American Baptist Publications Society 1894.

Scott, Jean Thomson. "The Conditions of Female Labour in Ontario." In W.J. Ashley, (ed.) *Toronto University Studies in Political Science*, First Series III. Toronto: Warwick and Sons 1892.

Schudson, Michael. *Discovering the News — A Social History of American Newspapers*. New York: Basic Books, Inc. 1978.

Showalter, Elaine. *A Literature of Their Own — British Women Novelists from Bronte to Lessing*. Princeton University Press 1977.

————. "Feminist Criticism in the Wilderness." In Elizabeth Abel (ed.) *Writing and Sexual Difference*.

Smith-Rosenberg, Carroll. *Disorderly Conduct: Visions of Gender in Victorian America*. New York: Alfred A. Knopf 1985.

Socknat, Thomas P. *Witness Against War: Pacifism in Canada 1900-1945*. Toronto: University of Toronto Press 1987.

Somerville, Edith and Martin Ross. *The Real Charlotte*. Virginian Beards (ed.) Rutgers University Press 1986.

Spender, Dale (ed.) *Men's Studies Modified: The Impact of Feminism on the Academic Disciplines*. Oxford: Pergamon Press — The Athene Series 1981.

Splane, R.B. *Social Welfare in Ontario 1791-1893*. Toronto: University of Toronto Press 1965.

Stamp, R.M. *The Schools of Ontario*. Toronto: University of Toronto Press 1981.

Stoddard, Jennifer and Veronica Strong-Boag. "...And Things were Going Wrong at Home." In *Atlantis*, Vol. l, No. 1. Fall 1975.

Strasser, Susan. *Never Done—The History of American Housework.* New York: Pantheon Books 1982.

Strong-Boag, Veronica. *Parliament of Women: The National Council of Women of Canada 1893-1919.* Ottawa: National Museums of Canada 1976.

———. "Canada's Women Doctors: Feminism Constrained." In L. Kealey, (ed.) *A Not Unreasonable Claim.*

———. "Setting the Stage: National Organization and the Women's Movement in the late 19th Century." In Alison Prentice and Susan Mann Trofimen koff (eds.) *The Neglected Majority*, Vol. I.

Sutherland, Neil. *Children in English-Canadian Society: Framing the 20th Century Consensus (1880-1920).* University of Toronto Press 1976.

Tauskey, Thomas (ed.) *Sara Jeannette Duncan Selected Journalism.* Ottawa: Tecumseh Press 1978.

———. *Sara Jeannette Duncan, Novelist of the Empire.* Port Credit, Ont: P.D. Meany Co. 1980.

Traill, Catherine Parr. *The Backwoods of Canada.* Intro. Clara Thomas. Toronto: McClelland and Stewart 1984.

Trask, David F. *The War With Spain in 1898.* New York: McMillan Publishing Co., Inc. 1981.

Trofimenkoff, Susan Mann. "One Hundred and Two Muffled Voices—Canada's Industrial Women in the 1880's." In *Atlantis* Vol. 3, No. 1. Fall 1977.

Turcotte, Dorothy. "Kit Coleman—A Gutsy Female—Pioneer Journalist." In *Early Canadian Life*, Vol. 3, No. 4, May 1979.

Walkowitz, Judith R. *Prostitution and Victorian Society—Women, Class and the State.* Cambridge University Press 1982.

Walsh, H.H. *The Christian Church in Canada.* Toronto: The Ryerson Press 1968.

Weaver, Emily. "Pioneer Canadian Women-'Kit' the Journalist." In *Canadian Magazine*, Vol. 49, No. 4. August 1917.

Whitridge, Margaret Coulby. "The Distaff Side of the Confederation Group: Women's Contribution to Early Nationalist Canadian Literature." In *Atlantis*, Vol. 4, No. 1. Fall 1978.

Williams, Vicki L. "Home Training and the Socialization of Youth in the Sentimental Novels of Marshall Sauders, Nellie McClung and L.M. Montgomery." Unpublished M.A. thesis, Carleton University 1982.

Willison, John. *Reminiscences Political and Personal*. Toronto: McClelland 1919.

Wisan, Joseph E. *The Cuban Crisis As Reflected in the New York Press (1895-1898)*. New York: Octagon Books 1965.

MAGAZINES, PERIODICALS AND NEWSPAPERS

Canada Monthly, Feb. 1911-June 1915.

Canada West Magazine, April 1909.

Canadian Magazine, 1898-1917.

Stratford, (Ont.) *Daily Beacon*, Feb. 1911-July 1912.

Toronto *Daily Mail*, 1889-Feb. 1895.

Toronto *Empire*, 1890-Feb. 1895.

Toronto *Globe*, 1885-1915.

Grain Grower's Guide, 1912-1917.

Grip, Vol. XXXVI, No. 3 (17 Jan. 1891); No. 4 (24 Jan. 1891).

Hamilton (Ont.) *Herald*, 1911-1915.

Toronto *Mail & Empire*, Feb. 1895-June 1915.

Vancouver *News Advertiser*, 1912-1915.

New York Herald, 7, 14, 21, 28 June 1891.

New York Times, 3 July 1898.

Rose-Belford's National Annual Review (previously *Canadian Monthly and National Review*), 1875-1882.

Saturday Night, Aug. 1889-June 1915.

Hamilton (Ont.) *Spectator*, May 1915.

Montreal Daily *Star*, 1885-1915.

Toronto Daily *Star*, 1902-1915.

The General Federation Clubwoman, Sept. 1898; March 1900.

The Week, 1889-1896.

The Western Home Monthly, July 1906.

Toronto *World*, 1909-1915.

ARCHIVAL HOLDINGS AND OTHER DOCUMENTS

National Archives of the United States, Records of the Military, RG 107; RG 64.

N.W. Ontario, Manitoba and N.W. Territories Directory and Gazetteer 1886-1888.

Provincial Archives of Manitoba, Florence Randal Livesay Papers. P59.

Public Archives of Canada, Kathleen Blake Coleman Papers, MG 29 D 112. Finding Aid No. 1724.

Public Archives of Canada, Media Club of Canada Papers, MG 28 I 232. Finding Aid No. 1006.

Public Archives of Canada, John Willison Papers, MG 30 D 29, Finding Aid No. 158.

Public Archives of Canada, Ships' Passenger Lists 1884, Microfilm C4533.

Queen's University Archives, W.W. Campbell Papers. 2001b B09f003.

Queen's University Archives, Lorne Pierce Collection 20016 B032f008, Hale-Garvin Papers.

Royal Commission on the Prison and Reformatory System in Ontario (1891), Ontario Sessional Papers, No. 18.

Saskatchewan Archives Board. Katherine Simpson Hayes Papers. Microfilm #2.15.

Thomas Fisher Rare Book Library, the University of Toronto, F.M. Denison MS. Collection 51.

Toronto City Directory 1884-1885, 1889-1915.

ORAL HISTORY

Mr. J.B. Gartshore and Mrs. Kit Waterous. Interview conducted in person by Barbara M. Freeman at Ancaster, Ontario, 7 Dec. 1987.

Sister Eleanor O'Meara, Archivist, Loretto Abbey, Toronto. Interview conducted by telephone from Ottawa. Barbara M. Freeman, 13 July 1989.

INDEX

World, New York 82
World, Vancouver 138
Wyse, Winnifred M. 20